Sociology: A Very Short Introduction

VERY SHORT INTRODUCTIONS are for anyone wanting a stimulating and accessible way into a new subject. They are written by experts, and have been translated into more than 45 different languages.

The series began in 1995, and now covers a wide variety of topics in every discipline. The VSI library currently contains over 550 volumes—a Very Short Introduction to everything from Psychology and Philosophy of Science to American History and Relativity—and continues to grow in every subject area.

## Very Short Introductions available now:

**Available soon:**

For more information visit our website

www.oup.com/vsi/

Steve Bruce

# SOCIOLOGY

## A Very Short Introduction

SECOND EDITION

OXFORD
UNIVERSITY PRESS

# OXFORD
UNIVERSITY PRESS

Great Clarendon Street, Oxford, OX2 6DP,
United Kingdom

Oxford University Press is a department of the University of Oxford.
It furthers the University's objective of excellence in research, scholarship,
and education by publishing worldwide. Oxford is a registered trade mark of
Oxford University Press in the UK and in certain other countries

First published as an Oxford Paperback 1999
Reissued 2000
Second edition published 2018

Published in the United States of America by Oxford University Press
198 Madison Avenue, New York, NY 10016, United States of America

British Library Cataloguing in Publication Data
Data available

Library of Congress Control Number: 2018943458

ISBN 978-0-19-882296-7

Printed and bound by CPI Group (UK) Ltd, Croydon, CR0 4YY

# Contents

# Preface

It is a sign of the power of sociology that it is both popular and reviled. Longer-established academic disciplines deride it as a brash newcomer but adopt its perspectives. Ordinary people mock those who pursue it professionally yet take many of its assumptions for granted. Conservative governments accuse the discipline of undermining morality and social discipline yet hire sociologists to evaluate their policies.

Our unease with the discipline can be seen in the frequency and the nature of the jokes. This may be professional paranoia, but it seems that there are sociologist jokes in a way that there are not historian jokes. As humour does not translate well I will recount just one. This gem came from the British television series *Minder*, a fine 1980s comedy of minor villains and London low life. Two lovable rogues are discussing a mutual acquaintance who has just been released from prison. One announces that their friend has been improving himself while inside by studying: 'Yeh. He's got an Open University degree now. In sociology.' The second asks: 'Has he given up the thieving then?' and the first replies: 'Nah! But now he knows why he does it!'

This is a complex jibe. Sociology appeals to villains (presumably because it often studies social problems). By showing the social causes of individual action, sociology absolves people of responsibility. Sociology is naïve and can be manipulated by the worldly wise. Whether the discipline is guilty of any or all of these charges should be clear by the end of this short introduction.

For reasons that will become apparent, social scientists find it harder to agree than do natural scientists. Researchers at the leading edge of physics, for example, may argue ferociously, but there is sufficient consensus among ordinary physicists for introductory physics textbooks to state with authority the basic knowledge that is accepted by the trade and must be acquired by entrants. In contrast, introductory social science texts often describe their subjects as a series of competing perspectives. There are some benefits to stressing such divisions. By taking specific emphases to their logical conclusions, we can readily perceive the arguments that need to be resolved if we are to explain this or that facet of the social world. Like politicians in elections, advocates of particular schools try to put 'clear blue water' between themselves and their rivals. But fortunately, also like politicians in power, when they get round to doing sociology, they tend to fall back on common ground.

The narrow constraints of this *Very Short Introduction* format free me from the obligation to map the discipline comprehensively. Instead I will convey the distinctive essence of the sociological vision. This will be done in three stages. First, I will explain the status of the enterprise by considering what is meant by describing sociology as a social science. In Chapters 2, 3, and 4 I will try to explain some of its fundamental assumptions. In Chapter 5 I will try to clarify the sociological enterprise by distinguishing it from some unfortunately popular impostors.

# Acknowledgements

I must thank Gordon Marshall (Director of the Leverhulme Trust and formerly of Nuffield College, Oxford and the University of Reading), and George Miller of Oxford University Press for suggesting I write this book. Gordon Marshall, Steven Yearley of the University of Edinburgh, and David Inglis of the University of Exeter were kind enough to comment on early drafts. Roy Wallis of the University of Stirling and the Queen's University of Belfast was responsible for my early sociological education. David Voas, of University College, London, did much to persuade me of the enduring value of treating sociology as a social science. Hilary Walford's copy-editing of the first edition removed many of my initial errors and Dan Harding similarly improved this second edition. I am grateful to all of them.

# Chapter 1
# The status of sociology

## Sociology and science

For as long as we have been impressed by our understanding and control of the material world, scientists and philosophers of science have tried to specify what distinguishes successful modern scientists from alchemists trying to turn stone into gold and astrologers trying to predict our futures from the positions of the stars. Unfortunately, all such attempts have failed to produce unambiguous lines of demarcation, and, when we have looked closely at what scientists actually do, we often find that the working life of science fails to match the picture painted by the philosophers. Nonetheless, we can list a series of characteristics that are more likely to be found in physics than in alchemy and in astronomy than astrology. While we cannot with absolute certainty divide science from pseudo-science, we can profitably talk about things being 'more or less' scientific and we can contrast science with everyday reasoning.

A good starting point is that any good scientific theory should be internally consistent. This immediately separates it from lay reasoning. My opinionated mother contradicted herself more often than not. That something she said one moment was incompatible with her next pronouncement never troubled her. She once

1

criticized a roadside café by asserting that the food was vile and the portions were too small!

A good scientific theory should fit the evidence. This may seem obvious, but what the scientist should demand in this respect is considerably more rigorous than that which the lay person habitually accepts. Very different standards operate, for example, in conventional and in alternative medicine. Although driven by commercial imperatives to get their drugs to market before those of their rivals, pharmaceutical companies subject their products to lengthy and extensive trials. In 'double-blind' testing, large numbers of patients are divided into test and control groups. One is given the new drug; the other a harmless and inert placebo. Until the allocations are revealed at the end of the trials, neither patients nor doctors know who is getting the real drug and who the placebo. Only if the test sample shows a marked improvement over the placebo group is the trial accepted as evidence of the drug's efficacy. In contrast, alternative therapies such as faith healing, acupuncture, or magno-therapy are rarely tested; the personal experience of the practitioner, supported by a few unsubstantiated anecdotes of miracle cures, is taken to be sufficient. Such testing as takes place is never extensive or double-blind. Thus the twin possibilities that some patients 'get better' because common maladies resolve themselves and that any treatment may produce a placebo effect—we get better because we expect the therapy to work—are never eliminated.

Third, science constantly changes. Its findings are never true in an absolute now-and-forever sense; they are always provisional and can always be improved. The convincing orthodoxy of one century becomes the historical curiosity of the next. It is a little awkward to say that science makes *progress*, because that suggests we know where we will end up, but we certainly know where we have been, and can thus talk about science gradually moving away from error. Again we can see the point if we contrast the reliance of medical science on experimental proof with the reliance of alternative therapies on tradition. In the world of Bachian flower remedies, Feng Shui, and Shiatsu massage, that something has been done for centuries (preferably in a culture untainted by modernity) establishes its validity. Given that such fundamentals of medical science as the body's circulatory system are relatively recent discoveries, the scientist is rightly not impressed by the age of an idea.

In bad science (such as Erich Von Däniken's claims that the Egyptian pyramids were built by visiting spacemen) theories are supported by snippets of fact plucked out of context. In good science the key to the replacement of one explanation by another is the systematic collection of *extensive* data that bear on the matter. But this is not enough. Few ideas are so bizarre that no evidence can be found to support them. Reasons to believe are easy to find. A much more telling test is to search for reasons not to believe. In good science the most persuasive ideas are those that survive repeated attempts to prove them wrong.

This brings us to one of the most important features of science: the way it deals with failure. Imagine I develop a new theory about subatomic particles. In my laboratory, assisted by students whom I have trained in my perspective, I generate lots of experimental observations to fit my theory. But then scientists elsewhere repeat my work and fail to confirm my findings. I should reconsider my theory in the light of the new evidence. If my theory can be refined to encompass the new results or to explain why the new observations are misleading, then it stands. If not, it should be ditched.

The value of this approach is most easily seen if we consider an alternative. A client comes to a witch doctor with a skin rash. The witch doctor poisons a chicken, and, from the way it staggers before dropping dead, determines that the rash has been caused by the client's sister-in-law bewitching him. The client is given a charm and told that, if he wears it for a week, the spell will be broken and the rash will clear up. But a month later the rash is as bad as ever. Instead of concluding that the idea that illness is caused by evil spells is nonsense and that the charm lacks curative power, the witch doctor explains that the client did not have enough faith: the cure will only work when the client truly believes.

Though this illustration is taken from African traditional medicine, modern scientists can be similarly inventive in saving their pet theories from refutation. Clearly science would be best served by practitioners being strongly committed to the enterprise in general but not being overly attached to their own particular theories. But scientists are only human. What saves science from reliance on the saintly detachment of individual scientists is *competition*. The person who has spent twenty years developing a particular theory may work hard to defend his or her ideas. However, the career structure of natural science means that there will be many others in the same field who see career advancement in proving their elders wrong.

Science thrives on the free exchange of ideas and on intellectual competition. It stagnates when, as in the Middle Ages under the Catholic Church or in the 1930s Soviet Union under communist party rule, an outside agency imposes an orthodoxy that is not rooted in the work of the discipline. In the 19th century some geneticists argued that characteristics that individuals acquired during their lifetimes could be passed on through their genes. French biologist Jean-Baptist Lamarck believed that the giraffe owed its long neck to the habit of stretching to reach leaves on tall trees. The counter-case would suppose that 'long-necked-ness' was already a genetically encoded quality and that those giraffes that possessed it had a better chance of survival (and hence breeding) than those that did not. So genetic stock changes through 'natural selection' rather than learning. By the 1920s the Lamarckian view had been largely abandoned. However, it survived in the Soviet Union, where the natural selection alternative was thought to be too close to the logic of capitalism and hence politically unacceptable. Trofim Lysenko used his political position to have Lamarckism incorporated in official communist philosophy, and those geneticists who opposed him were either forced to recant or exiled to Siberia. Only in the 1950s did Soviet biology recover from Lysenko's influence.

It is now fashionable to deride the idea that the scientific method guarantees truth. Sociology has itself played a significant part in undermining the grander claims of science by showing that its ways of working are often similar to the mundane methods ordinary people use to make sense of the world and that scientists are not immune to interests and values that compromise their claims to detachment. Nonetheless, modern science has been so successful in allowing us to understand and manipulate the natural world (far too successful, many critics would say) that it offers an obvious place to start when we consider how we might study the social world. That is, it is not an accident that, in most university structures, sociology is to be found, not with 'arts and humanities', but in faculties of 'social science'.

## Can sociology be scientific?

However, if we begin our description of the sociological enterprise by saying that it should model itself on the methods of the physical sciences, we cannot proceed very far before recognizing some fundamental limits to such imitation.

The first is that social scientists can rarely experiment. While researching Protestant terrorist organizations in Northern Ireland in the 1980s, I became interested in how certain people had come to occupy important leadership roles. Having found out everything I could about the leaders (and about those who might have been regarded as leadership material but never made it), I came to a number of tentative conclusions. Contrary to what one might expect of terrorist organizations, it was not personal viciousness that kept leaders in office. Out of some thirty cases, I could find only two people who had ruled by fear. One of them was murdered by his own people as soon as his more senior protectors had lost office; the other would have been had he not been arrested and imprisoned. More important than naked coercion was the ability to persuade and reconcile. However, this skill seemed to be common among leaders across the twenty-five years of the conflict, which left unexplained a major difference in the background of those who commanded in the 1970s and those who replaced them in the mid-1980s.

While diplomacy was a general requirement, social status was important for the first decade but not thereafter. The first generation of leaders were almost always people who had occupied some sort of community leadership role *before* the violence broke out. They had held office in trade unions, community associations, political parties, and housing associations. The men who came to prominence in the late 1980s were very different. Most had grown up in the terrorist organizations and had come to the fore because they were 'operators': effective killers and planners of robbery, extortion, drug-dealing, and the like.

The differences between the generations led me to this somewhat obvious conclusion. In a new enterprise, where no one has relevant experience or can point to a track record, general marks of status or competence are used to select leaders. Leadership is taken to be a 'transferable skill'. But once an enterprise has been going long enough for large numbers to have gained experience of its core activities (in this case, planning or carrying out murders and related criminal acts), then it becomes possible to judge potential candidates for leadership on those skills. The attention shifts from very general marks of competence (such as having been prominent in some other community activity) to more specific task-related attributes.

This explanation could be wrong. What matters for my purposes here is how I could further test my idea. The chemist studying bromide reactions could devise further experiments that held constant what were taken to be extraneous variables and changed only those things that were thought to be central; the effects of those changes could be measured and compared. But I could not, for experimental purposes, create a stable society and then engineer a civil war. Even were it were possible, no reader should need persuading that the pursuit of social-scientific knowledge cannot justify terrorism. However, let us imagine that both ethical and practical obstacles had been overcome. Creating my own terror group would still not have produced data comparable to those from the repeated experiments of the bromide chemist, because my terror group would not have been the same as the 'naturally occurring' ones I wished to understand. There are two problems. One is that artificial experiments in the social sciences have a fundamentally different relationship to the real world than chemistry experiments because the social experiment is not a facsimile of the naturally occurring: it is itself a novel social event. The other issue is that social life is often too complex to be broken into component parts that can be examined in isolation.

So one major difference between the natural and social sciences is that the ideas of the latter cannot normally be rigorously tested by experiments that isolate what interests us from the complexities of ongoing life. However, we can and often do perform quasi-experiments by systematically comparing settings that are mostly similar but different in just one or two key ways. The work of Rosabeth Kanter on utopian communities provides a good illustration. She wanted to know why some communes succeeded while others failed. Her extensive reading of the history of such groups and her own involvement in the communes of the 1960s had given her some general ideas about which features of such engineered societies might work. So she began with some hypotheses, derived from previous scholarly work and shaped by her own unsystematic observation, and then sought a test of those ideas. To avoid the effects of differences in the communities being swamped by differences in their surrounding societies, she concentrated on communes that had been formed in one country within a relatively short time period: in this case, the United States between 1780 and 1860. She managed to identify ninety such communities: eleven 'successes' that had survived twenty-five years (the conventional view then of a generation) and seventy-nine 'failures' that had not lasted a quarter of a century. She concluded that, although there were no properties present in all the successes and entirely absent from the failures, some characteristics were common in the successes and rare in the failures. The successes demanded considerable sacrifice (such as abstinence from sex, alcohol, and dancing) from their members. They had worldviews that drew hard divisions between the good people of the commune and the rest of the world. They had very strict definitions of membership and rigorous membership tests. New members were required to prove their commitment by investing a great deal of time and money in the enterprise, which in turn made it costly to defect. Almost all the successes bolstered this psychic and social separation from the world with geographical isolation. Kanter concluded that commitment was not a mysterious phenomenon that preceded the formation of a utopian community. Rather it was a social property that could be engineered by the deliberate use of what she called 'commitment mechanisms'.

Researchers since have modified Kanter's conclusions. I have argued that it is easier to engineer commitment to some sorts of belief systems than to others. Those political philosophies and religions that vest supreme authority in individual followers are far more difficult to organize than those that evoke some God or higher power: the difference between herding cats and herding cows. Conservative Catholics and Protestants can form successful communities; liberal Protestants and devotees of New Age spirituality cannot. However, here I am more interested in Kanter's method than in her conclusions. She very ably demonstrates that, while we cannot experiment as easily as the natural scientist, with some imagination we can find examples from real life to simplify social phenomena.

Social scientists routinely do this with large-scale social surveys. Imagine we want to know what effect gender has on political preferences. We could ask large numbers of men and women how they voted in an election and compare the answers. However, if we stopped there we would learn very little, because other characteristics such as income, levels of education, race, and religion also affect political preferences. So we ask our men and women further questions that allowed us to assign them labels for levels of income, years in formal education, ethnic identity, religious affiliation, and so on. We then use the statistical method of multivariate analysis to work out which of these characteristics, either on its own or in combination, has the greatest effect on voting.

While such research is illuminating, its conclusions are always tentative and probabilistic. We can say with confidence that in industrial societies working-class people are more likely to lean to the left politically than the upper classes. But there are enough exceptions to that proposition to stop us treating it as if it were a natural law. In the West in the 1950s it was possible to identify 'deferential workers' who, though objectively working class, were nonetheless extremely conservative in their politics and supposed that their social superiors would make a better job of running the country than would the representatives of the workers. In the 1980s the neoliberalism promoted by Margaret Thatcher in the UK and Ronald Reagan in the USA—laissez-faire on economics but authoritarian on social issues—drew strong support from blue-collar workers in affluent areas. So we start with a simple expectation and find that it needs to be refined. Simple divisions of people by gross types of occupation (such as manual and non-manual work) are not powerful predictors of voting. So we further divide class or we add other considerations, but we find that our propositions never move beyond probabilities.

Some sociologists take such failures as encouragement to become more sophisticated in the definition, identification, and measurement of what are taken to be the causes of social action.

While improvement in those three areas is all to the good, sociology's failure to produce laws reflects far more than its relative immaturity. After 150 years of scientific sociology, the 'it's early days yet' defence sounds rather thin. More data collection and analysis will make us better informed, but we will never discover the laws of human action because people are not like atoms.

The social sciences study sentient beings who act out of choice. At this stage we do not need to get bogged down in familiar arguments about the extent to which people are really free. All we have to recognize is that, whatever the sources of uniformity in human behaviour (and more of that later), they are not absolutely binding. The most oppressive regime may reduce our choices to conform or die but we can choose death. This radically distinguishes people from the subject matter of the natural sciences. Water cannot refuse to have its volatility increased as it is heated. With pressure held constant, water cannot boil at 100°C for four days and then refuse to do so on the fifth day. People can. Even the lowest worm can turn.

This leads us to recognize that what counts as explanation in the social sciences is not like explanation in physics or chemistry. We explain why the kettle boils by citing the general laws of pressure, temperature, and volatility. Because the water has not *decided* to boil (a decision that it could change on some other occasion), we do not need to refer to the consciousness of the water. If we wish only to identify some very broad regularities of human behaviour, then we can treat social characteristics like the variables of natural science and propose, for example, that unskilled workers are more likely than businessmen to vote socialist, but if we wish to *explain* why that is the case then we have to examine the beliefs, values, motives, and intentions of the people in question. Because the human consciousness is the engine that drives all action, the social sciences have to go further than the natural sciences. When the chemist has repeatedly found the same reactions in his bromides, he stops. Identifying the regularity is the end of that search. For the social scientist it is only the beginning. Even if we found that everyone in a particular situation always did a particular thing (and such invariant regularities are almost unknown), we would want to know *why*.

The words 'what' and 'why' neatly expose the difference. For the chemist they can be the same thing. When chemists have collected enough data under the right controlled circumstances to be confident they know what happens, they also know why it happens. But when the German sociologist Max Weber collected enough information to persuade himself that there was some strong connection between the spread of the Puritan branch of the Protestant Reformation and the rise of modern industrial capitalism (the 'what' issue), he had only begun. He wanted to know why the Puritans developed a set of attitudes that were particularly conducive to modern entrepreneurial methods. He wanted to know why a particular set of religious beliefs could have created a novel attitude to work and to consumption. He sought the answer in the minds of the Puritans. In order to explain, he had to understand.

The sociologist's interest in beliefs, values, motives, and intentions brings with it concerns unknown in the natural sciences. To understand people, we need in some manner to solicit their views or accounts of what they are doing. Furthermore, we can take the same point back one step and note that it is not just understanding that requires some interest in motives. Even identifying the social act we wish to understand requires attention to motives. The ways of defining when a liquid changes to a gas make no reference to its state of mind. But the actions of people cannot be known simply by observing them. Or, to put it another way, the physical action itself is not enough. Suppose we are interested in how people interact in public places. We sit at a table in a crowded railway station and watch and take notes. But if we confine ourselves only to what was visible, we learn little. We note 'man facing platform raises arm in air and moves it from side to side'. We cannot say

11

'man waves to greet incoming passenger', because that description gives a particular interpretation, based on a guess about intention, to the physical action. He might actually be trying to relieve a trapped nerve or restore blood flow.

For simple acts performed by people of our own culture, we can often assume we know their significance. I have met enough people off trains to know 'waving' when I see it. But suppose the action involved kneeling and lowering and raising the body with the arms outstretched. In Peking, it might be a form of exercise. In Cairo, it might be a prayer. In the end the only way to ascertain the meaning of the action is (by some method or another) to ask the person 'What are you doing?' Even the identification of actions requires some attention to intentions.

Even more so does their explanation. In one way or another, the sociologist ends up having to ask people about their motives and intentions. But asking and being asked are themselves pieces of social interaction. The accounts that people give can be knowingly false: people lie. More commonly accounts are simultaneously honest attempts to reconstruct past motives and current performances through which people pursue present interests and the two things are may be difficult to separate.

In some settings the distortion is obvious. We can be sure that what the accused say in court before the verdict or sentencing will be quite different to the version they give to friends and family after they have been found 'not guilty' or happily avoided a custodial sentence. The person telling the story has interests in the outcome of the telling and the court itself requires stories to be told in an unusually stylized manner. We know there is a standard form to courtroom testimony because counsel can coach witnesses. I am not saying that the courtroom version is always false and the informal version always true. What I am saying is that giving an account is itself a novel social activity shaped by its context and the interests at play; it is not merely an explanation of earlier activities.

Another example can be drawn from religious conversion stories. It is common for converts to 'witness' to their faith by recounting their experience of conversion. One need hear only a small number of these testimonies to realize that they follow a few common templates. The convert was raised in the faith by godly parents who did their best to keep the child on the straight and narrow, but the temptations of the world were too great, and the child fell into a life of sin. Whatever pleasures that life produced gradually turned sour. Some precipitating crisis (often the death of the saintly mother or another loved one) brought the convert 'under conviction of sin'. American Protestants are very fond of road stories: 'As I drove home that night, I felt a weight of sin pressing on me. I realized that if I died then I was going to hell. I stopped the car and prayed for Jesus to come into my life.' The day and the time and the place are stated. In the final paragraph of the story, the convert relates how much his life has changed for the better since he gave himself to the Lord. Now, it may be that such testimonies are very similar because the underlying reality they describe is similar. But, given that anyone raised in an evangelical Protestant culture will have heard hundreds of such stories, it is always possible that the similarities stem from the popularity of the narrative form. That is, the well-known narrative shapes the way people experience their lives.

I repeatedly encountered a version of this problem in my interviews with Loyalist paramilitaries in Northern Ireland. Some people, probably from reticence well ingrained from years of resisting police interrogation, deliberately downplayed their role in terrorist crimes. Others, presumably to enjoy shocking a middle-class academic, exaggerated their crimes. One man was so keen to brag of his deeds that he claimed a murder I knew he had not committed. The problem of the research interview itself distorting the evidence it seeks to collect is not confined to research on crime and other obviously sensitive subjects. It pervades every kind of social investigation, because the act of investigation introduces new variables.

To give just one example, public-opinion pollsters used to ask people how they felt about this or that and report their answers without considering that the very fact of asking people for their opinions might lead them to assert feelings about things of which they knew nothing and cared even less. One Californian survey slipped in a question about an entirely fictitious issue that was supposedly to appear on a forthcoming referendum. Respondents were asked 'You will have heard of the Snibbo amendment. How do you feel about it?' and they were given the usual range of responses. A large proportion claimed to be either for or against, many of them strongly so. Perhaps they felt they would look foolish if they admitted they had no idea what the interviewer was talking about. Perhaps they were trying to be helpful. Perhaps the nature of the interaction ('Here I am answering questions') led respondents to get so firmly into the way of giving definite responses that inertia carried them over what they should have seen as a break in the tracks.

What people say and what they actually did might be linked in four ways. First, respondents may not recall or understand their motives. Second, they may recall or understand all too well but deliberately dissemble. The 19th-century industrialist John Pierpont Morgan hit on an important point about the desire to appear decent and honourable when he said: 'For every act there are two reasons: a good reason and the real reason.' Third, whatever the level of self-understanding and willingness to be honest, the setting for the giving of accounts may exert such an influence that we cannot with confidence use what people say as a guide to their previous mental states: individual variety might be funnelled into apparent consensus—the conversion testimony is an example.

14

Between these last two types, we can place a fourth case: collective dissembling. Often a group of people share what for them are good reasons for their actions but routinely explain what they do by calling on a publicly more acceptable language of justification. For example, doctors may ration expensive treatments for renal failure or lung cancer by informal moralizing about what sort of person *deserves* their attention (and we can guess that it will not be alcoholics or smokers), but then avoid having to defend such reasoning by claiming that decisions were made solely on sometimes related but sometimes quite different grounds of the likelihood of the intervention being successful.

One possible response to the variable relationship between why people act and what they later say about their actions is to give up trying to understand what Harold Garfinkel disparaged as 'what goes on in people's heads'. The more radical of Garfinkel's students argued that we cannot in the conventional sense *understand* people. All we can do is study the mechanics of account-giving. Thus we can analyse the formal structures of courtroom talk but we cannot use that talk to determine guilt. We can describe religious conversion testimonies in the same way that we can analyse an orchestral score, but we cannot use them as data to explain conversion.

This is an unwarrantedly pessimistic conclusion. Sociology has no magic that, if correctly performed, separates information that leads to understanding from misleading dross. But, equally well, courts sometimes arrive at the truth; skilful interrogators penetrate obfuscatory defences; people discover their lovers have been cheating on them; and opinion pollsters find ways of overcoming 'compliance effects'. For example, asking people 'Which of the following did you do last weekend?' and inserting 'Attend church or equivalent' in a long list of possibilities such as 'Play sport', 'Shop', 'Visit relatives', 'Go to the cinema', and the like produces a lower figure for claimed church attendance than asking directly 'Did you attend church (or equivalent) last weekend?'.

That we have no single infallible technique for extracting truth from what people say does not mean that we cannot devise imaginative ways of circumventing the obvious problems and hence that we are bound always to fail. If ordinary people can sometimes draw warranted conclusions from speech, why not the social scientist?

So far the differences between the natural and social sciences have been discussed to the disadvantage of the latter. A different conclusion is possible. Long experience may make racehorse trainers confident that they can metaphorically put themselves in their horses' hooves. But social scientists begin with the great advantage of sharing biology, psychology, and a great deal of culture with their subjects. I have never been a member of a terrorist organization, committed a serious crime, or designed my life to minimize the chances of assassination or arrest. But I can find in my own experience causes to which I have been strongly attached, events that have caused me fear and anger, and actions of which I am proud and others of which I am profoundly ashamed. Even when those we study seem as distant as citizens of a foreign country, there is enough in our common humanity to create countless border-crossings. The medieval knight promising to build a chapel if he returns from the Crusades, the Trobriand Islands fisherman performing magic rituals before setting to sea, and the Italian footballer making the Sign of the Cross as he takes to the football pitch are engaged in recognizably similar activities and, if we could arrange time travel so that they met, we could be confident they would understand each other's evocations of divine assistance and rituals of reassurance.

When we fail to understand each other we often realize that fact and take steps to clarify. Whatever analytical purchase is lost by us not being able to experiment is amply regained by our ability to sustain extended conversations with our subjects. I could not test my ideas about terrorist career structures experimentally, but I could, directly and indirectly, raise them with my respondents. And I can draw on my understanding of myself to rough test social science explanations. We should always be cautious of applying to other people some explanation we would find implausible if applied to ourselves.

## Summary

We need to appreciate the differences between the subject matter of the natural and the human sciences. People think and feel. They act as they do, not because they are bound to follow unvarying rules but because they have beliefs, values, interests, and intentions. That simple fact means that, while some forms of sociological research look rather like the work of chemists or physicists, for the sociologist there is always a further step to take. Our notion of explanation does not stop at identifying regular patterns in social action. It requires that we understand. But whatever reservations we may have about how closely actual scientists conform to the high standards set in their programmatic statements about what they do and why it works, we need not doubt that the natural sciences offer the best model for acquiring knowledge. Critical reasoning, honest and diligent accumulating of evidence, testing ideas for internal consistency and for fit with the best available evidence, seeking evidence that refutes rather than supports an argument, and engaging in open exchanges of ideas and data unconstrained by ideological commitments; all of these can and should inform the social sciences.

# Chapter 2
# Social constructions

## Defining sociology

Most disciplines can be described by the focus of their attention or by their basic assumptions: we could say that economists study the economy or that they assume that a fundamental principle of human behaviour is the desire to 'maximize utility'. If we can buy an identical product in two shops at two different prices, we will buy the cheaper one. From that simple assumption an increasingly complex web is spun. For example, economists go on to assume that, as the price of wheat falls, so demand for it will increase and as the price of wheat goes up farmers will produce more.

Similarly, we could describe sociology as the study of social structures and social institutions, and sociological work is often divided into such topics as the class structure of modern societies, the family, crime and deviance, religion, and so on. However, to list what we study gives no sense of what is distinctive about the way we do it. This account of sociology will hang a number of substantial observations on a central thread made of the following strands: reality is socially constructed, our behaviour has hidden social causes, and much of social life is profoundly ironic.

## Humans create culture

When Darwin's theory of evolution seeped into popular culture, it became common to see humans as just big clever animals. At the start of the 20th century, the notion of instincts provided a popular way of explaining our actions. At the start of the 21st century, when gene mapping allows us to explain certain sorts of illness, the idea that human behaviour is determined by biology has again become popular.

An easy way to dismiss the more extreme forms of biological determinism is to point to the many ways we deliberately reject instincts. There may be a will to live, but we can commit suicide. There may be a will to reproduce, but women can choose not to have children and still live apparently fulfilled lives. There may be a sex urge, but celibacy is possible. The claims for biology are further weakened if we note the considerable cultural differences in what might be instinctual. Not only do people kill themselves but the suicide rate differs from one society to another, as does the frequency of childlessness and celibacy. Whatever part instinct plays in our lives, it is complicated by cultural variations.

Yet biology can provide a useful starting point because, if we understand how the biology of most animals determines their lives, and then appreciate the extent to which it *fails* to do so for humans, we can see the importance of culture. Ants do not ponder whether to follow the lead ant; their genes programme them to do so. Unlike women considering alternative maternity hospitals, salmon do not consider where might be nice to reproduce; they automatically return to spawn where they spawned before. In contrast, humans derive very little direction from their biology, which creates difficulties for the individual in terms of self-management and for the group in terms of coordination. As I will later explain, what follows is artificial in that it poses problems we have already solved. Nonetheless, the hypothetical problems let us appreciate the importance of the solutions.

Arnold Gehlen used the term 'world-openness' to contrast the enormous potential of the human condition with the limited opportunities enjoyed by other animals. Bulls can eat, walk, and run around, bang heads with other bulls, and mount cows that are in heat. And that is about it. Bulls cannot transcend the constraints of their environment. We can build towns under the Alaskan ice where those who extract oil from the frozen wastes can soak in a hot tub and watch films in a heated cinema. There is so much we *could* do that, without some guide as to what we *should* do, we would be paralysed by indecision. So we simplify by creating routines and forming habits. What worked one day becomes the template for action the next. We get up about the same time every day, eat the same sorts of things, and wear the same sort of clothes. By ignoring most of our possibilities and treating a large part of the rest as habits, we retain just a small area of the world for freely chosen thought-about actions.

But, even once habit-forming has reduced world-openness to something manageable, we would still be ruined by the inherent restlessness identified by French sociologist Émile Durkheim. He begins with the proposition that 'No living being can be happy or even exist unless his needs are sufficiently proportioned to his means.' For most other animals, such equilibrium is established 'with automatic spontaneity'. The ant's goals are simple and set by its biology. The extent to which it meets those goals is set by its environment. The ant is satisfied or it is dead. It makes no sense to talk of an unhappy or frustrated ant. As Durkheim puts it:

> When the void created by existence in its own resources is filled, the animal, satisfied, asks nothing further. Its power of reflection is not sufficiently developed to imagine other ends than those implicit in its

physical nature…This is not the case with man, because most of his needs are not dependent on his body or not to the same degree.

One consequence of our freedom from instinctual or environmental control is that, no matter how much we acquire or achieve, we can always want to have or have been more. Indeed success seems to stimulate further desire. I wanted transport. After much saving, I bought an old small car. For a while I was content. Then I began to resent being overtaken by everything else and yearned for a more powerful car. Once I got that, I wanted two cars: a saloon car for cruising highways and a four-wheel drive for bumpy country roads. Such frustration is partly a modern problem, a consequence of the weakening of traditional restraints. In part it is a result of desires being stimulated by advertising. But it is also a universal problem. What Durkheim wrote at the start of the 20th century refers to non-material goals as much as to material possessions:

> All man's pleasure in acting, moving and exerting himself implies the sense that his efforts are not in vain and that by walking he has advanced. However, one cannot advance when one walks toward no goal, or—which is the same thing—when his goal is infinity. Since the distance between us and it is always the same, whatever road we take, we might as well have made the motions without progress from the spot. Even our glances behind and our feelings of pride at the distance covered can cause only deceptive satisfaction, since the remaining distance is not proportionately reduced. To pursue a goal which is by definition unattainable is to condemn oneself to perpetual unhappiness.

The solution is *regulation*. A moral force, a shared culture, which specifies what we can desire and how we can attain it, replaces the biological straitjacket. To fill the gap left by what Gehlen called 'instinctual deprivation', people create social frameworks. Some parts of those frameworks may be fixed in formal law. The bulk of it is merely conventional. No law says that white-collar workers in management positions should wear dark suits, but aspirants to senior management know how to dress. At its most effective, the straitjacket is applied not to the outside of the body but to the inside of the mind. We are socialized in the culture so that important elements of it become embedded in our personalities.

If we can see the importance of culture in giving a framework within which the individual can achieve contentment, the third problem of world-openness—coordinating joint action—should be even more obvious. Where, as with ants and bees, communication and coordination are themselves biological, there is no difficulty. One ant does not need to interpret the signals given off by another. It responds automatically to the secretions. Even complex matters such as arranging the appropriate combinations of roles within a hive of bees are not debated by the bees. They respond automatically to the death of the queen bee by feeding another egg the genetic material which turns it into a queen.

## Roles

Human biology does nothing to structure human society. Age may enfeeble us all, but cultures vary in the prestige and power they accord to the elderly. Giving birth is a necessary condition for being a mother, but it is not sufficient. We expect mothers to behave in maternal ways and to display appropriately maternal sentiments. We prescribe a clutch of norms or rules that govern the *role* of mother. That the social role is independent of the biological base can be demonstrated by going back three sentences. Giving birth is certainly not sufficient to be a mother and, as adoption and fostering show, it is not even necessary.

The fine detail of what is expected of a mother, a father, or dutiful child differs from culture to culture, but everywhere behaviour is coordinated by the *reciprocal* nature of roles. Husband and wife, parent and child, employer and employee, waiter and customer, teacher and pupil, warlord and foot soldier; each makes sense only in its relation to the other. The term 'role' is an appropriate one, because the metaphor of an actor in a play neatly expresses both the rule-governed or scripted nature of much of social life and the sense that society is a joint production. Social life occurs only because people play their parts (and that is as true for wars and conflict as for peace and love) and those parts make sense only in the context of the overall show. The drama metaphor also reminds us of the artistic licence available to the players. We can play a part straight or, as the following from Jean-Paul Sartre conveys, we can ham it up:

> Let us consider this waiter in the café. His movement is quick and forward, a little too precise, a little too rapid. He comes towards the patrons with a step a little too quick. He bends forward a little too eagerly; his voice, his eyes express an interest a little too solicitous for the order of the customer. Finally there he returns, trying to imitate in his walk the inflexible stiffness of some kind of automaton while carrying his tray with the recklessness of a tightrope-walker... All his behaviour seems to us a game... But what is he playing? We need not watch long before we can explain it: he is playing at being a waiter in a café.

The American sociologist Erving Goffman built an influential body of social analysis on elaborating the metaphor of social life as drama. Perhaps his most telling point is that it is only through acting out a part that we express character. It is not enough to be evil or virtuous; to be seen as evil or virtuous we must act those parts.

The distinction between the roles we play and some underlying self will be pursued later. Here we might note that some roles are more absorbing than others. We are not surprised by the waitress who plays her part badly in order to show that she is more than her occupation. We would be surprised and offended by the father who played his part 'tongue in cheek'. And some roles are broader and more far-reaching than others. Describing someone as a clergyman or faith healer says far more about that person than describing someone as a bus driver. Here the main point I want to make is that, in the absence of strong biological linkages, reciprocal roles provide the mechanism for coordinating human behaviour.

## Order and orders

To prevent my line of argument from becoming confused with an apparently similar point, I will add this aside. Durkheim, Gehlen, and others who point to the social benefits of order and regulation are misunderstood when they are described as political conservatives. To see only their concern with stability is to miss the point. All human action, conservative or radical, reactionary or revolutionary, requires basic ordering. Thomas Hobbes worried that without some external power imposing civility, people would pursue their own interests to the detriment of the good of all. My point is that even such self-seeking requires a considerable amount of common culture. Even anarchists must stabilize their characters, communicate with each other, and understand the enemy.

We make life manageable by creating social institutions that do for us what instincts do for other animals. By routinizing programmes of action and either painting them onto the 'backcloth' of the stage on which we perform or writing them into a script, we can leave free for creative improvisation and conscious choice an area that is small enough for individuals and groups to manage without becoming overwhelmed.

However, though we may on calm reflection see the virtues of allowing large parts of our lives to follow well-worn paths, modern people periodically feel themselves frustrated by the impersonality and predictability of life. We do often try to distinguish between the social roles we play and the real 'us'. Like Sartre's waiter, we perform in such a way as to show to our audiences that we are more than, and can rise above, our roles as managers, civil servants, bus drivers, fathers, and loyal spouses. We may use hobbies, holidays, and weekend trips to establish a persona separate from our place in the paramount reality of everyday life.

However, and this reinforces Gehlen's case for the importance of shared order, even these escapes are commonplace and repetitive. Just as sheep without thinking about it will take the same least arduous route around a hill, so, even when we think we are engaging in daring, radical, and convention-defying acts, our lives tend to follow well-beaten tracks. The middle-aged businessman, bored with his wife and family, tries to rediscover his autonomy (and his youth) by having a fling with his secretary. He imagines he is an intrepid discoverer of the romantic alternative to the dull and mundane, but he merely embraces yet another well-worked script. In the metaphor elaborated by Laurie Taylor and Stan Cohen, he has climbed over the prison wall to what, for a while, he imagines is freedom, but he has simply fallen into the exercise yard of a different prison.

## The solidity of culture

This argument is one development of the idea that reality is socially constructed. Against those who suppose that the regularities in human action stem from our common biology, the sociological perspective begins by noting that humans differ from other animals in the extent to which their worlds are open and potentially unformed. Hence such regularities as we find (and we find them often because they are essential to the maintenance of psychic and social stability) are a product of culture: people make it up. And culture cannot be reduced to biology.

There is a further small but important version of this claim. Even when objective stimuli are implicated in our actions, it is our *interpretations* of those stimuli that affect our behaviour. Consider the way we get drunk. It is unlikely that there are major differences in the way the Australian Aboriginal farmer, the New York businessman, the Scottish medical student, and the Italian child metabolize alcohol, but there are huge variations in how these peoples behave when they drink. I do not mean just that cultures differ in attitudes to drunkenness, though they do: what is acceptable for a fishing crew returned from a week in the north Atlantic is not what one would expect at a business lunch in Edinburgh. I mean that the overlay of culture is such that different peoples *expect* alcohol to affect them in different ways and as a result do indeed feel different. The amount of alcohol that in one context produces staggering, incoherent speech, and incontinent giggling can in another produce quiet reflection and feelings of peace. Or, to put it another way, we learn what to expect and by and large find it. As Howard Becker argued in his seminal essay 'Becoming a Marijuana User', the same objective sensation could be interpreted as elation or nausea and learning to feel the former rather than the latter is a crucial part of becoming a dope smoker.

This brings me to an aspect of sociology that causes great difficulty for novices. It is tempting to divide the world into things that are real and things that are imagined: an objective external reality and subjective internal landscapes. One of my students, who lacked both a way with words and a sense of humour, managed to summarize criticisms of biological explanations of schizophrenia by saying 'So we can see that mental illness is all in the mind'! Possibly, but the realm that interests sociologists is neither 'all in the mind' nor entirely external to our consciousness: it is intersubjective. Things that people imagine, provided they are imagined similarly by large enough numbers of people, can have an enduring and even oppressive reality indistinguishable from the objective world. In considering how we explain our actions, the American social psychologist William Thomas wrote that, if people define situations as real, then they are real in their consequences. The man who believes his house is on fire will run from it. That the house does not burn down proves he was wrong,

but to understand his actions what matters is his belief and
not the truth.

The same point can be made on a much bigger scale if we
consider a social institution such as religion. Sociologists are
not in the business of deciding which religion, if any, is correct.
We need observe only that there are hundreds of religions, many
of which are basically incompatible. If Roman Catholics are
right, then Protestants, Muslims, Hindus, and Buddhists are
wrong. So we can accept minimally that one or more religion
is mistaken. Yet religious belief systems can be immensely
powerful. The Christian Church in the Middle Ages ruled states
and its beliefs shaped both high culture and the everyday lives of
ordinary people. Through its rituals, and the ideas expressed in
those rituals, the Church provided an accompaniment to birth,
marriage, and death, and to the cycle of changing seasons.
Although detailed theological knowledge was restricted to the
few people who were literate, almost everyone knew that there
was a God who had made the earth and heaven and hell, who
demanded certain types of behaviour, and who punished and
rewarded. Even the not-especially devout shaped their behaviour
to conform to the Church's interpretation of divine requirements
and had frequent recourse to the Church's magic. Blessed
amulets, holy water, relics of the saints, and a forest's worth of
pieces of the Holy Cross were both objects of veneration and
practical devices to improve health, social relations, and
agricultural productivity. I need not labour the point: whether
or not the medieval Christian Church had the 'true' religion,
people believed that it had and acted accordingly.

However, and this is the vital point, social constructions are viable
only to the extent that they are shared. Fabrications they may be,
but, if everyone believes them, then they are no longer beliefs;
they are just 'how things are'. A worldview that is shared by few
people does not attain that solidity: it remains belief. If it is shared
by very few or only one, it will be seen as madness.

So far I have simplified by supposing that what makes intersubjectivity solid is numbers: the views of the many are accurate descriptions while the views of the few are pathologies to be rejected or remedied. This is important, because a worldview gains enormous plausibility from the unremarked repetition of mundane acts that embody it. When, as in the Middle Ages, the response to every danger is to make the Sign of the Cross and every misfortune is met with prayer, when every parting is solemnized by saying 'God be with you' (the original of the English *Goodbye*) or 'I commend you to God's protection' (for the French *Adieu*), and when good weather is greeted with 'The Lord be praised', then the idea that the world was created by God is simply taken for granted. In this way, consensus gives great power to culture. But it is worth pointing out that not all views are equally powerful or persuasive: individuals and social groups differ in their ability to 'define the situation'. As Peter Berger put it: he who has the biggest stick has the best chance of imposing his views. We might add that what counts as a stick varies from society to society.

Most societies are not content to leave the plausibility of their culture to the weight of consensus. To use the term popularized by Karl Marx, they also *reify* (from the Latin *re*, a thing, meaning 'to make thing-like'). If Gehlen and Durkheim are right that culture does for humans what instinctual and environmental constraints do for other species, then we must often choose to remain blind to its human origins. If we openly acknowledge the socially created nature of our arrangements and are too familiar with the fact that other peoples do things differently, our institutions lose conviction and we are back in the uncomfortable position of world-openness or anomie.

In practice we have a wide variety of devices for reification. To give an example from the purely personal level, an elderly female acquaintance of mine does not 'drink coffee'. Instead, at the same time every day, she has 'coffee time': a formulation that implies she is adhering to a timetable not of her own devising. Her coffee breaks are presented as an obligation. 'Coffee time' requires not only coffee but a biscuit, because 'a drink is too wet without one'. As someone who has spent very little of her long life in paid employment, her schedules are very obviously her own choices, yet she sees her life as a series of scheduled obligations and even, just sometimes, derives pleasure from rebelling against them.

On a grander scale, we can observe that most societies seek extra legitimation for their institutions. Primitive hunters supposed that they hunted in this particular way because that was how the Pig Gods taught them to hunt. Medieval monarchs claimed divine support for kingship. The Victorian hymn writer who composed 'All Things Bright and Beautiful', with its lines 'The rich man in his castle, the poor man at his gate, God made them highly and lowly, and ordered their estate', had the specific intention of persuading the poor to accept their situation, and there is no doubt that the repeated singing of that popular hymn did something to discourage the lower orders from getting uppity.

Just as societies differ in their sources of power, so they also vary in what can be claimed as additional legitimation for particular social arrangements. As in the three examples just given, religious societies ascribe authorship to God or gods. In 19th- and early 20th-century Western Europe, when religious explanations became less persuasive, people started to claim scientific justifications for particular orders. So it was no longer God who had ordained the estates of the rich man and the poor man but their genetic material or, as neoliberal economists would have had it, the mysterious but invincible rules of political economy. That societies differ in just who or what is thought to have created the social order concerns me less than this abstract point: the near-universality of reification suggests that it serves a purpose greater than merely bolstering the powerful.

There is one good reason why reification is so common: it contains a basic truth. None of us personally created the social institutions that shape our lives; we were born into them. The roles that structure our behaviour and encapsulate the expectations that others will have of us preceded our arrival in this world and will endure (no doubt slightly modified) long after we depart it. Reality may be socially constructed, but, taken in its totality, it is not the work of any nameable individual and it certainly has little or nothing to do with any one of us. Language is a good example of the coercive nature of conventions. Of course it is devised by people, but its basic shape is presented to us. Though we may modify it (and one or two of us may actually author a significant change), our general sense is that we simply adopt and conform to what is already in place.

To summarize, we can recognize that reality is socially constructed without supposing the reverse: that if we stop defining a situation as true then it will melt away like snow on a hot dog's back. Social institutions have enormous power. Simply 'de-constructing' them by showing their human origins (especially by showing that some groups benefit more than others from particular institutions) will not make them vanish.

## Layers of construction: people at work

Religious organizations have a habit of claiming that their structure is divinely ordained, but government agencies, commercial corporations, factories, and other 'formal organizations' readily admit their human authorship. Often we can name the people who created a particular organization or radically altered its structure. Yet even in this field sociology can be radical in identifying discrepancies between rhetoric and reality, or between what the formal structure is supposed to look like and how it actually works. We can take the notion of social construction as an invitation to appreciate the difference between the original architect's drawings for a building and what was actually built.

An old but still perfect example of this sort of study is Melville Dalton's *Men Who Manage*. To appreciate the importance of

Dalton's work we should step back to Max Weber's writings on bureaucracy. Each member of the founding trinity of sociology had one big idea of how modern societies differed from their predecessors. For Marx, it was class. For Durkheim, it was the breakdown of shared norms. For Weber, it was the rise of rational organization. I should here add a qualification that applies to all the contrasts given in this book. Though it simplifies our stories if we pretend it does, social development does not fall into neatly demarcated periods. There are very few clean breaks. Attitudes and habits common in one period give way to others only gradually, and many will survive in particular geographical regions and social groups. When sociologists talk about social change in terms of epochs, they are, like caricaturists, identifying and amplifying the most significant features of a society. If space permitted, everything said here would be accompanied by many qualifying details and exceptions. But it does not, so I will press on with the sweeping generalizations.

In a small group of people linked by ties that endure over long periods of time and over many areas of business (which is what we mean by the term 'community'), interaction can be monitored and coordinated face-to-face. Awkward people can be informally criticized and, if that does not work, shunned or ostracized. Decisions can be arrived at by negotiation and consensus. As the small community is replaced by the large-scale society, both the numbers of people involved and the complexity of the matter in hand require a very different form of management. Twenty subsistence farmers sharing common grazing can meet frequently to decide how many beasts each can graze on the common. The allocation to multinational firms of blocks of the North Sea for oil exploration and extraction requires formal organization.

One feature of modernization is the massive increase in rational bureaucracy. Bureaucracy is not an invention of industrial societies; as Weber notes, the ancient and medieval Chinese were rather good at it, and for most of twenty centuries the Christian

Church has been bureaucratically organized. But Weber believes that modern societies differ from traditional ones in the extent to which life is dominated by rationality.

More will be said about this in Chapter 4; here I want to summarize Weber's account of modern organization. First, the modern bureaucracy distinguishes between the office and the individual who occupies it. When the sheriff or the chief executive resigns, the power passes to the next holder of the office. The distinction between office and occupant also applies to rewards. The assets of an engineering company belong to the company and not to the official who happens currently to be managing director. As an incentive we may offer officials shares in the company, but generally they are paid a salary that is independent of its assets. To see how things could be arranged differently, consider the medieval institution of tax farming. Candidates for the position of tax collector offered to raise competing amounts of money for the king. The successful bidder could collect as much as he liked over and above what he had offered to deliver. This was effective in raising revenues for the king but it encouraged tax collectors to bleed taxpayers. The tax revenues of modern democracies are quite separate from the salaried income of the officials who collect them.

Second, the bureaucracy handles its affairs after the fashion of the division of labour in manufacturing. Complicated business such as fighting a war is broken down into component parts so that for every job there is one, and only one, responsible office. The armaments section organizes the production of weapons; the medical corps treats the wounded; the pay office arranges for soldiers to be paid; and so on. As well as ensuring that everything that needs to be done is done and is done only once, this division of labour allows officials to become expert in their specialized business. It also means that new officials can be trained and tested in the specific skills needed for the job, and expertise can determine promotion. Within task sections, offices are arranged in a clear

hierarchy with unambiguous chains of command. All officials
know to whom they answer and who answers to them. Finally the
work of officials is shaped by rules that are applied universally.
All cases (for they are 'cases' rather than people) are dealt with
in the same way and are judged only on the matter in hand.
Modern tax collectors do not charge their friends, relatives, and
co-religionists less than they charge strangers; they apply the
same rules to all taxpayers.

At first sight and at a distance, this model offers an entirely
convincing account of a major difference between modern and
traditional societies. The German Army in 1900, the Church of
England after its 19th-century reforms, or the US Internal
Revenue Service provide ample illustrations. However, Weber's
depiction also reads like a public relations exercise in that it
presents an idealized picture.

Dalton's scepticism about the rationality of modern organizations
stemmed from his own experiences as a junior manager in two
US manufacturing firms. While doing his job, he observed how
he and his colleagues worked. He concluded that there was a
considerable gulf between formal procedures and actual operations.
The prevailing ideology of management in those days was that it
was 'scientific', following essentially rational methods to the
single best solution for a problem. Dalton shows management
to be a self-interested political activity, involving negotiation,
compromise, and the recognition that very few problems have a
single optimal solution. Dalton penetrates the idealized business
school model to expose the reality: managers negotiate practical
solutions to problems and then, when necessary, deploy the
rhetoric of formal organization to justify decisions that were
actually made on often different pragmatic grounds.

I will give just three illustrations. One company tightly controlled
spare parts and materials, which could be signed out of the store
only on the production of a docket that identified the job for

which they were required. However, the production line managers
wanted to keep spare stock on hand to minimize costly delays.
To discourage such hoarding, the company required unannounced
audits of stock. The people who checked on the production
managers also needed to work amicably with them. So, before
an inspection the checkers leaked the time and the route. The
production managers kept their illicit supplies on trolleys so
that they could be quickly hidden. Thus the checkers met the
organization's formal requirements while maintaining good
relationships with the production staff and letting them get on
with their jobs.

Dalton was also interested in appointments and promotions.
He discovered that a disproportionate number of senior managers
were members of the Masonic Lodge and also members of the
Yacht Club. They had apparently been appointed, not just for their
expertise, but also because they were 'one of us' and were able to
informally bargain and exchange to get things done. They were
also members of respected informal cliques. Although these
characteristics were not part of the formal criteria for management
selection—indeed, they were outlawed as discriminatory—Dalton
shows how, from the management's point of view, they made
practical sense.

A third example of the gulf between rhetoric and reality
concerns the hierarchy of authority and the power of offices.
The companies for which Dalton worked followed Weber's
model of having an apparently unambiguous structure of who
answered to whom and clear demarcations of remit. However,
some of the managers who formally shared the same status were
more influential than others. Lower officials knew which of their
superiors were of little account and could have their jobs dealt
with last and which were 'coming men' who should be given
preferential service. In part this reflected competence; not all
holders of formally equal offices were equally good at their jobs.
In part it was a reflection of commitment. One man was close to

retirement and wanted a quiet life while another was young and ambitious and took every opportunity to increase the power of his office. In the language of Goffman's drama metaphor we could say that, as for Shakespeare's *Hamlet*, the parts were scripted but the actors retained considerable freedom in the way they acted out the role.

That the reality of a complex organization did not mirror its formal structure is no longer a surprise. We are now well used to the point Dalton makes, but that it is now a truism does not stop it being true and important. Apparently well-defined formal organizations are constantly shaped and reshaped by the activities of those who inhabit them. This is not to say that they are chaotic and disorganized. It just means that the original theorists of formal organizations mislocated somewhat the *site* of formality. Dalton's companies functioned well because they were defined by reasonably clear goals (though these were sometimes in conflict) shared by managers and workers who created and maintained shared practical understandings of how to do the business and who also knew how, if called upon to account for themselves, to present their actions *as if* they followed logically from the formal structures and operating procedures.

## Layers of construction: rule-breakers

That reality is repeatedly reconstructed in layers can be illustrated with the example of law and law-breakers. There is no doubt that law is a human product. Books of political science and jurisprudence can name the people who make it. In the United Kingdom, Parliament makes the law. In the United States, Congress makes federal law while the legislatures of the states make state law. In addition we can note that, although judges and justices are supposed only to interpret and apply, their applications can themselves create new law. In some cultures—Iran under the ayatollahs, for example—supernatural legitimation is sought for the law by claiming that it is divinely ordained, but even here we can identify the ayatollahs whose interpretation of the Quran has shaped the *Sharia* or religious law.

We can take the existence of the law as our starting point and suppose that we can readily read off what will count as law-breaking. We identify a particular act—man forces his sexual attention on woman—and, by holding it up to the template of the law, see if it is criminal or not. Unfortunately, it is not so simple. In the first place many laws are in themselves ambiguous. Even very detailed laws cannot specify how they are to be applied in every currently conceivable case or in circumstances yet to be encountered. Second, many acts are potentially governed by many laws and the fit between them is not always neat. Laws accumulate. Framers may do their best to harmonize new and existing legislation, but there will inevitably be clashes, so that, even when the act in question is not contested, what laws should be used to judge it may well be.

Furthermore, laws are rarely applied consistently. On British trunk roads, the default speed limit is 60 miles per hour. However, traffic police very rarely stop people between 60 and 65 miles per hour because measuring equipment and car speedometers are not accurate enough to be sure of intent to disregard the limit. But even this new 'real' limit is not applied evenly. My local police force has more calls on its time than it can meet and speeding on country roads is low priority. On a quiet day, a traffic team will park behind a row of trees on a straight section where motorists habitually exceed the limit and book a few miscreants before going back to more pressing matters. Thus the chances of being caught speeding depend on the press of other calls on police time. Additionally, how the police react to a speeding driver will depend not only on such facts of the matter as speed and road conditions but also on such intangibles as the driver's attitude and demeanour. If the motorist appears to be the sort of person who does not habitually disregard speed limits, then a stern word is the most likely sanction. If the driver is rude or 'seems like a speeder', then a booking and fine are more likely. In deciding how to respond, the police ask not only 'Has an offence been committed?' but also 'Is this person a typical offender?'

So we begin with the simple formula that crime is that which breaks the law and quickly discover that the matter is considerably more complicated. Indeed there seem to be so many filtering layers of decision-making and interpretation that we might more accurately say (a) that crime is what police decide breaks the law and (b) that such decisions include many extra-legal considerations. This would already be a significant elaboration on our starting point, but, of course, the police are not the only people who have a part in identifying criminals. The prosecuting authority has to decide whether to prosecute or not, and, if so, for what offence. Judges and juries have to try the case and arrive at a verdict.

A criminal justice system is a complex process of repeated social constructions, with each element driven by its own interests (as well as by respect for the law in the abstract) and with each element influenced by decision-making at other stages. The police handling of domestic violence offers a good example of such feedback. In the 1960s the British police commonly ignored 'domestics'. They justified this by noting that the victims often refused to give evidence in court and that courts often failed to convict or only handed down light punishments. For police forces with more than enough business to consume their resources, domestics did not seem worth the trouble. However, this began to change in the 1970s when organized women's groups managed to draw media attention to violence in the home. This, in turn, influenced judges, who became less tolerant of it. New arrangements were devised to reduce the stress on complainants (at the investigation and prosecution stages), which in turn led to more complaints being made, to witnesses being more willing to give evidence, and to the police calculation of 'reward for effort' changing in favour of more robust action. So we gradually see the social constructions of domestic violence changing.

The idea that there is a large body of family crimes of violence, of which a shifting proportion gets reported, recorded, processed, and tried, still assumes that the raw material of the justice process is a world of acts that unambiguously divide into criminal and not criminal. However, a more radical view is possible. If it is the case that the 'actual' status of the original act has less bearing on the final outcome than the various considerations that intervene at the filtering stages, it may be more accurate to say that the acts of social definition or *labelling* are actually the source of criminality. A moral philosopher or a policeman may want to say that crime-ness is a property of original acts, some of which are discovered while others go undetected. If we are interested in the social consequences of actions in the real world, it might be better to see it as a property of the labels that official definers attach to certain acts.

The labelling perspective on crime and deviance, which became popular in the late 1960s and obviously owed much of its appeal to its apparently radical attitude to social order, is most convincing when applied to ambiguous and borderline cases. A rugby club dinner results in considerable damage to a hotel; is this youthful high spirits or serious hooliganism? An elderly lady believes that aliens have taken over her TV set; is this eccentricity or mental illness? A small shopkeeper massages his tax returns; is this fraud or entrepreneurial flair? The body of a fisherman is found tangled in his boat's rigging; is this suicide or accidental death? Given that there is obviously a lot of room for arriving at quite different interpretations of these acts or events, the labelling approach seems justified. It has the great advantage of drawing our attention to the fact that the final labels may owe as much to creative interpretation as to discovery. And it allows us to see the range of interests involved in such interpretations.

We can hazard the following guesses. Criminal damage done by the upper-class rugby club will be defined as 'high spirits', whereas the same acts committed by football fans will be regarded as vandalism. If the elderly lady is financially independent and is not a key figure in a family, her oddities are more likely to be tolerated than to become the focus for treatment. The businessman who cheats to preserve 'his own money' from the taxman will be less severely punished than a social security fraud who steals 'other people's money', even if each similarly damages the common good. If the deceased fisherman has relatives and belongs to a conservative religious tradition, his ambiguous death is more likely to be judged accidental than if he is single and secular. In all these examples we can see that whether a particular act is judged to be a crime or to be deviant is not fully explained by any quality of the act itself and that other considerations enter into the process of labelling or social definition.

However, important though this is in giving us a more realistic account of crime and deviance, the labelling approach exaggerates by neglecting two important points about social definitions. First, some social rules are actually quite simple and enduring. In any particular society or subculture there may be such consensus that we can leave aside the process of social definition identified as central in the labelling approach. While some brutal physical contacts can be explained away ('he fell down the stairs') and others justified ('I thought he had a knife and was going to attack me'), there remain many cases that very few of us would have difficulty correctly labelling as assault with a deadly weapon, grievous bodily harm, murder, and the like. While a wide range of strange behaviour can be tolerated as eccentricity, a similarly wide range would with little hesitation be taken as symptoms of madness requiring therapy. That is, although we know that something is a crime or is deviant only because it is defined as such by society (the labelling point), in any particular society in any particular decade, such definitions may be so well established and understood that they are fairly evenly applied by most people. I do not mean that the guilty never get away with it; I mean that we would have little difficulty agreeing that a certain person did get away with it.

Second, the labelling perspective overlooks conscience. This allows me to introduce the idea of *internalization*. At its most robust, the labelling approach means that the crime that goes unlabelled by others is not a crime. Yet ten years after he had killed his wife and buried her under the patio, a man walked into a police station, asked to talk to a detective, and confessed. He did so because he was tormented by guilt. He did not need any external authority to label his act a crime; his own conscience had already done that. Although his socialization into the norms of his culture had not been so complete as to prevent him killing, it had been sufficiently effective to prevent him being at ease with his action. He had labelled himself as criminal. And while diagnosis as mentally ill can be seen as the external imposition of a label, very many of those so diagnosed have actively sought treatment.

Talking of conscience allows me to restate a point implicit in the first section of this chapter: humans become social when the external contours of their culture are replicated inside their minds and their personalities. To return to the theatrical metaphor used earlier, in a stable society the actors do not just read through their parts. They are 'method actors' who have been so thoroughly steeped in their parts that they live them. The external aids of script, stage directions, and prompts are no longer necessary: the actors have taken on the characters.

A large part of sociology is concerned with trying to understand how that happens. One of the key principles of sociology is that how people see themselves is greatly affected by how others see them. I have already identified one large-scale version of this phenomenon when I talked about society as a system of interlocking roles. To be a father requires that there be sons and daughters. To be a teacher requires that there be students and pupils. To be a good father requires that sons and daughters think of you as a good father and that others (spouse, grandparents of your offspring, friends, and neighbours) share this view.

This can be put in personal dynamic terms when we appreciate the part that the responses of others play in *learning* a role. A man tentatively acts in ways he thinks appropriate to a good father. He then reflexively monitors the responses of his children and of others close to him who observe those performances, and modifies his actions in the light of how he thinks others see him. If he senses approval, he can take pride and pleasure in what he has done. When he sees hostility, lack of understanding, fear, and loathing, he may feel ashamed. The American social psychologist Charles Horton Cooley coined the phrase 'the looking-glass self' to describe this process of acquiring an identity by responding to what we see of ourselves in the eyes of others. Sometimes such monitoring is formal and overt: the man and his wife may argue about the principles of good parenting. More often the monitoring is so low key as to be almost unconscious.

An important consequence for identity of social interaction is that attempts to identify who or what someone is can become *self-fulfilling*. If a young girl repeatedly fails to tidy her room, be ready on time, and collect the appropriate equipment for even simple tasks, her father may repeatedly depict her as an 'airhead': cute but incompetent. If this sort of designation and its implied explanation is repeated sufficiently often, by both parents and other close relatives and friends, the girl may well come to internalize that image of herself. She learns to think of herself as incompetent and comes more and more to act the part. What was intended as an accurate description of existing character actually creates what it thought it had observed.

A number of important qualifications need to be added to this account. First, the person being labelled is rarely passive. Identity is *negotiated*. The girl may find ways of responding to her father's view of her other than simply accepting it and conforming to the implied expectations. Her father, in turn, may find new ways of understanding her behaviour that, for example, turn 'airhead' into 'spiritually aware child'. Furthermore, not all of those who interact with the girl will be equally influential. George Herbert Mead talked of 'significant others'. For the child, parents (or their surrogates) will be the most significant others, but older friends and other relatives can also be influential. In later life people who occupy formal positions become significant and we may even be influenced by the supposed views of abstract 'reference groups'. When I was a graduate student I wrote with the imagined voice of my supervisor muttering criticisms in my ear; now, as I write this, I am mindful of the likely responses of the imagined community of professional sociologists.

A large body of research in the sociology of education very effectively uses the self-fulfilling prophecy to explain how schools inadvertently reproduce social class. We know from repeated surveys that children of working-class parents have a much higher chance of themselves ending up in manual work than the children of middle-class parents. We also know that this remains the case even when we compare children with the same IQ levels. Yet we also know that few teachers consciously discriminate against lower-class children or deliberately give them undeservedly poor marks. So how is class reproduced?

The answer is, of course, complex. The rich can buy additional resources (extra tutoring, for example) for their children. Housing patterns tend to reflect social class, so that local schools vary in class composition. Schools in good areas attract better teachers and gain reputations for good discipline and good exam results, which in turn makes an area more attractive to middle-class parents (and to some working-class and ethnic minority families whose ambition for their children makes up for what they lack in background and resources). Parents who have themselves succeeded in formal education both consciously and unconsciously pass appropriate attitudes and skills to their children. But, even recognizing those large background considerations, it remains the case that, within any school, the performance of the children tends to be influenced by class.

The explanation lies in a vicious circle. Working-class children (boys especially) begin with low expectations. They generally aspire only to the sorts of jobs done by their parents and close relatives and, not having succeeded in formal education, those parents are not well placed to encourage or assist their children. These same role models may inhabit a macho culture that leads their children to be louder and rougher than middle-class children. They tend to be somewhat disruptive even when they have no intention of being so. They work less well and, even when they work as well as other children, their virtues may be overlooked because teachers quickly form an estimation of how certain sorts of children will perform, and those expectations are based on subtle cues that have subtle social class components. In many often unconscious ways, those expectations are fed back to the children, so that they have a sense of failing even before they come to formal tests of achievement. The expectations are further reinforced in school systems where children are tested and judged at a very early age.

Once children start patently to fail, they have a choice. Either they can conform to the official value system of the school and see themselves as failures, or they can seek other sources of self-esteem. The latter is an option if children who have already experienced failure have created an oppositional subculture of kids who pride themselves on acts of rebellion and who enjoy 'taking the piss out of the teacher'. One boy at my school (in the days when physical punishment was commonplace) fell foul of the staff early on, was belted unusually often, and came to take pride in being so hard that no one could break him. In his confrontations with staff he deliberately upped the ante in order to prove that no one could belt him often enough or hard enough to make him cry. Not surprisingly, staff quickly came to view him as a problem to be managed and he left school at the earliest opportunity with no formal qualifications.

What we have here is a situational theory of learning. It supposes that those who feel devalued because they are judged to be failing in one particular system of values may be drawn to a counter-culture which reverses the dominant values. In order to feel good about themselves, the poor boys become the bad boys in a deviant subculture in which 'bad' is cool.

The above draws on the social psychology of Mead and Cooley to suggest that consistently treating people as if they were a certain sort of person may make them just that. However, we can tell a slightly different version of the same sort of story in which the actor's acceptance of the judgements of others is less important. Let us suppose a middle-management accountant is wrongly accused of fraud. Despite protesting his innocence, he is convicted and imprisoned. He loses his job, wife, children, home, and financial security. On release from prison he finds that he can no longer work as a straight accountant. He is shunned by former friends and associates. The exclusion from straight society contrasts with the acceptance he finds from criminals. In jail he mixed with people who admired rather than despised supposed crimes. Though he continues to deny his guilt he finds that there is a society of people who respect him for what he is supposed to have done. In those circumstances our accountant may well find himself open to offers from criminals. Instead of dissuading him from further crime, the fact of having been labelled a criminal may be sufficient to make him what, if we believe his protestations of innocence, he was not. In summary, whether or not the original tag was earned, certain kinds of labelling have considerable consequences because those who do the defining have the power to impose their definitions.

The labelling approach is not just an abstract perspective; it underpins juvenile justice systems. Although societies differ in what age they use as the cut-off, most modern states handle the crimes of young people so as to minimize the chances of them being pushed out of conventional roles and into criminal careers. Courts protect the identities of young offenders and, if they must be incarcerated, segregate them from adult prisoners who could provide unfortunate role models.

I would now like to return to the general theme of this section. What these discussions of crime and deviance, and of educational failure, show is that the creative element in social action is not confined to the birth of some institution. We cannot acknowledge that culture is a social product and then suppose that we can study social life without repeated reference to the creative interpretation that such a proposition implies. Instead we have to appreciate that social order is constantly fluid, ever in flux. While there is much value in understanding societies as collections of interlinked roles, guided by bodies of rules, we must always remember that the performance of some roles offers considerable scope for improvisation and the process of interpretation never stops.

# Chapter 3
# Causes and consequences

## Hidden causes

In Chapter 2 I made the obvious point that, while reality is socially constructed, it nonetheless has an enduring and oppressive quality because the personal part that most of us play in that construction is trivial. Even our conscious rebellions against order tend to follow preordained lines. One of the ways that sociology differs from common sense is in challenging our fond image of ourselves as authors of our own thoughts and actions. Captains of industry, religious visionaries, and political leaders may see themselves as free spirits but most of us have a pretty good idea of just how much autonomy we really possess. Nonetheless, our sense of identity presupposes that there is an 'I' independent of the ebb and flow of social forces. I may not be able to prevent my standard of living being affected by changes in bank interest rate but, within my means, I decide my diet, my political preferences, my religion, and my musical tastes. The other party will have a say in whom I love, but my end of the relationship is my choice.

Yet, if there is to be any explanation of human behaviour, there must be regular patterns to even those parts of life which we think we control and those regularities will be—at least partly—caused by forces outside our control and our cognition. The paradox between freedom and constraint was neatly expressed by Karl

Marx when he said that we make our own fate but not in the circumstances of our own choosing. The 'making our fate' bit is easy to see, as are the more immediate constraints. Although I decide where to drive on a Sunday afternoon, the manner in which I drive is shaped by traffic regulations and by the behaviour of other motorists. That is obvious to me if I care to think about it. But much of who we are and what we do has social causes that are obscure to us. By searching for regular patterns and by systematic comparisons between worlds, the sociologist can illuminate those causes.

A good example of research that finds social causes of what we take to be highly personal behaviour is the link between love and social identity. In many societies marriages are arranged by parents who select partners for their children with an eye to the value of alliances between families. Most modern people pride themselves on being free from such extraneous considerations and suppose they select purely on the nebulous but strongly felt emotional grounds of love. Those who continue to use the older form can serve as jokes. *Blind Date* was a popular television show format of the 1990s (since frequently repeated with small variations) in which an eligible young man or woman selected a date from contestants of the other gender who could be seen by the audience but not by the person choosing. The only information the selector got was a few jokey answers to jokey questions. The resulting date was filmed and the pair were invited back to a subsequent show to talk about each other. In Britain a number of Jewish businessmen floated the idea of founding a Jewish television channel. When asked about possible content, one of them joked that the channel might feature a version of *Blind Date* in which the contestant's mother gets to pick the date.

To the modern mind, it would seem a betrayal of true emotion to chose a spouse on the grounds of wealth, education, or career. Yet when we analyse such characteristics of spouses we find that choices supposedly made on the grounds of love and affection actually show very clear patterns of 'assortative mating'. While rarely conscious of (and even more rarely, admitting to) compromising love with extra-emotional considerations, most people marry others of the same religion, race, class, and educational background. In part this is a matter of opportunity: we are most likely to meet people who are like us. But it is also a matter of subtle indoctrination: our social groups effectively socialize us to see particular dress and hair styles, modes of demeanour and address, accents and vocabularies as being more attractive than others. Although the choice seems personal, what draws us to one person (or repels us from another) is much the same as what a diligent matchmaker would bear in mind when choosing a mate for us.

The same point can be made about many of our beliefs and attitudes. We may believe that we hold our views because we have dispassionately examined the evidence and come to the correct appreciation, but social surveys show repeatedly that much of what we believe can be predicted from such social characteristics as gender, race, class, and education. One might have thought that being religious was a highly personal matter, but in every industrial society (and in many others) women are clearly more devout and pious than men, however one measures those properties. Where a religious culture has a wide variety of competing organizations, most of them will have fairly clear racial, ethnic, and class identities. Activities associated with New Age spirituality (such as yoga and meditation) are much more popular with university-educated middle-class women who have worked in such caring professions as teaching, nursing, and physiotherapy than with working-class men or with middle-class men who work in business and commerce. The one exception is divination. Ill-educated working-class women are much more likely than their middle-class counterparts to have consulted crystal ball-gazers, palmists, astrologers, and other predictors of the future.

Of course, not everyone always wishes to claim ownership of his or her actions. No modern discussion of the extent to which we are shaped by social forces would be complete without some mention of the value of claiming victimhood. In any society there will be times when people wish to deny responsibility for their actions. Religious people blame divine displeasure or satanic influence. Secular cultures take a psychotherapeutic view; we blame our parents or attribute our character and behaviour to our genes. Or we can blame society. If Durkheim is right that the suicide rate for a society is determined by the twin social properties of 'regulation' and 'integration', then the responsibility of any individual for his or her suicide must be limited. Even more so in Marx's model of social evolution through class conflict. If we are what we are because of our relationship to the means of production (our 'class') and if we are borne along by the dynamics of class conflict, then we can hardly be held accountable for our fate. The interactionist sociology of Mead and Cooley, seen in its most radical form in the labelling theory of crime, similarly frees us from our own actions. If we become what others accuse us of being, then it is their fault, not ours.

Such popularized versions of sociological explanations are the lifeblood of those confessional and confrontational television talk shows in which sad people blame everyone but themselves for their petty tragedies. If you cannot maintain satisfactory personal relationships, that is because your father abused you as a child. Even if you did not recall being abused, the theory of 'rediscovered memories' allows you to claim that he actually did, although you did not know it until an abuse therapist helped you to introspect in middle age. Drug addicts, alcoholics, bulimics, anorexics, and sex addicts line up to claim social causes of their problems. There is perhaps no surprise in this. I will say more later about the relationship between the individual and the social roles he or she plays, but the fact that we can separate the person and the social role allows us to be self-interestedly selective in which actions or characteristics we wish to own and which we dismiss as the product of social conditioning.

Professional sociology differs from its lay counterpart here in a number of ways. First, it aims to be even-handed and disinterested. Ordinary people usually wish to blame society for their troubles but claim their successes for themselves. Sociologists are as interested in the social causes of health, wealth, success, and happiness as they are in illness, poverty, failure, and misery. Second, it aims to be led by the evidence. Third, it is concerned with the general and the typical rather than with the individual. Of course, the only way we can study the experiences of the typical unskilled industrial worker, for example, is by collecting information about hundreds of individual industrial workers, but it is the common elements, not the unique parts, of their experiences which concern us. The lay person draws on supposedly general principles of human behaviour to understand his or her life; the professional studies individual lives in order to generate the general principles.

## Unintended consequences

An important element of the sociological perspective is the irony of unintended consequences. As the Scottish poet Robert Burns succinctly put it: 'the best laid plans of mice and men gang aft aglay'; or, in English, 'often go wrong'. We set out to do one thing. Because we lack complete knowledge of the forces at play and because we cannot always anticipate how our actions will be received by others, we end up achieving something very different. I will illustrate the point with two examples that concern the links between ideas and the organizations that people create to promote those ideas.

Robert Michels, a student of Weber who was active in left-wing politics in Germany in the first decade of the 20th century, was struck by a common pattern of evolution in left-wing trade unions and political parties. They began as radical attempts to reconstruct the world but became increasingly conservative and at peace with the status quo. They began as primitive democracies but gradually evolved hierarchies. In an apparently different

arena—the world of conservative Protestant sects—H. Richard
Niebuhr identified a similar pattern. The Methodist movement in
the late 18th century was radical. Like the contemporary Muslim
fundamentalist who wishes to rid Islam of its blasphemous
compromises, Methodists broke from the Church of England
because they wished to return to a more pristine Christianity.
Initially they preached the restructuring of the world but
gradually became socially conservative. Initially they argued
against a professional clergy (because it relieved ordinary people
of the obligation to be personally pious), but gradually Methodist
Church officials came to exercise the same power as did the
clergy of the Church of England.

That a similar pattern is repeated suggests that it is not accidental
and can be explained by reference to some general social
processes. That the consequences were so different from what
those involved desired suggests that we cannot explain them
simply by obvious intentions and motives.

The explanation Michels proposed went as follows. Any kind of
group activity requires organization. But that creates a division
between the organized and the organizers; the latter acquire
knowledge and expertise that set them apart and give them power
over ordinary members. The officials begin to derive personal
satisfaction from their place in the organization and seek ways of
consolidating it. They acquire an interest in the organization's
continued prosperity. For ordinary trade unionists, the union is
just one interest in which they have a small stake; for the paid
officials it is their employer. Preserving the organization becomes
more important than achieving its goals. As radical action may
bring government repression, the apparatchiks moderate.

At the same time as material interests dispose them to compromise
their once radical credentials, the officials are drawn into new
perspectives because they acquire a new reference group. They
come to see that they share more in common with officials

of other political parties than with their own rank and file. Like servants discussing their masters, Labour and Conservative party activists swap stories about the idiocies of the people they represent and they exchange recipes for organizational efficiency.

Niebuhr's account of the decline of radicalism in Protestant sects is similar. The first generation of members deliberately and voluntarily accepted the sect's demands; they made sacrifices for their beliefs. Those who dissented from the state church in England in the 18th and early 19th centuries sometimes suffered political, social, and financial penalties. The state could confiscate their property and exclude them from a variety of public positions. The founding generation of sectarians invested more than just their hopes in the new faith, and their commitment, thus tested, was all the greater. But subsequent generations did not join voluntarily. They were born into it, and, however much effort was put into socializing them into the sect's ideology, it was inevitable that they would be less committed than their parents.

This was even more so the case if the sectarians, by working diligently to glorify God and avoiding expensive and wasteful luxuries, had achieved a standard of living considerably more comfortable than that of their own parents. The descendants of most first-generation Methodists were upwardly mobile and so had more to lose by their deviance. They mixed with others of more elevated status than their parents. They were a little embarrassed at the roughness and lack of sophistication of their place of worship, their uneducated minister, and their rough folk hymns. They began to press for small adaptations towards a more respectable format, more comparable to that of the state church.

There is a further point that mirrors exactly what Michels noted about political parties. Although most sects began as primitive democracies, with the equality of all believers and little or no formal organization, gradually a professional leadership cadre emerged. Especially after the founding charismatic leader died, there was a need to educate and train the preachers and teachers who would sustain the movement. Activities had to be coordinated, assets safeguarded, and books published and distributed. With organization came paid officials and such people had a vested interest in reducing the degree of conflict between the sect and the surrounding society. The clergy of mainstream churches became the crucial reference group: the sect's clergy came to feel they deserved the status and levels of education, training, and reward enjoyed by their more professional peers.

Niebuhr saw the sect as a short-lived form of religious organization, gradually becoming more tolerant, lax, and more upwardly mobile, and eventually becoming a denomination. This pattern can readily be found. It often takes more than one generation, but the Methodists in the fifty years after John Wesley's death fits the picture, as do the Quakers in the late 18th and 19th centuries. The austere commitment of early followers, with their distinctive mode of plain dress (with wide-brimmed hats for the men, who conspicuously refused to show respect for social superiors by taking them off) and distinctive forms of speech, gave way to more conventional styles. The early Quakers would not have read a novel or attended the theatre but their grandchildren, now wealthy merchants, manufacturers, and bankers, became more and more like the Church of England neighbours with whom they mixed as social equals. By the middle of the 19th century one finds them crossing over into first the evangelical wing and then the mainstream of the Church of England.

The Niebuhr pattern captures an important truth but it needs certain qualifications. Niebuhr concentrates on pressures for change within the sect and underestimates the influence of its environment. The rise of a professional clergy and a bureaucratic structure is often described as though it followed from moral weakness when it is in large part thrust upon any group in the modern world by the expectations of the rest of the society. As Weber argued, professionalism and bureaucracy are just the means by which modern societies organize things, and many sectarians find themselves obliged by the need to negotiate with the state (the right to be avoid military service, or to avoid property taxes that funded a state church they rejected, for example) to become more centrally organized.

Further, Niebuhr exaggerates the extent to which Protestant sects are much of a muchness. As Bryan Wilson has argued in detail, doctrinal differences between sects make them variously susceptible to the sort of accommodation Niebuhr describes. We need not pursue the differences further than noting that, precisely because people have self-awareness and can learn from their history, sects can try to organize themselves and their relations with their surrounding society so as to remain sectarian for many generations. Like most social patterns, the drift towards the denominational compromise is common but it is not inevitable.

These examples neatly illustrate the reverse consequence of the human capacity for reflexive thought. People can call on sociological explanations to provide justifications for their behaviour, and to console themselves if they cannot or will not change. But they can also learn from their past mistakes and from sociological accounts of their actions. Although Michels' conclusions are commonly titled 'the iron law of oligarchy' and Niebuhr's thesis is often treated as if it had similarly identified a basic law of social evolution, these are not laws in the natural science sense. It may be rare but it is possible for anarchists to avoid the pull towards compromise and respectability. Radical political movements can remain true to their initial ethos, even when it results in their destruction. Sects can resist the pull to denominational respectability. Communitarian sects such as the Amish and the Hutterites have maintained their distinctive character for two centuries by finding ways to avoid the more obvious pitfalls. In the first place, they created prohibitions on the use of modern farming machinery and thus kept down their productivity. When, despite this, they became wealthy, they used the profits to buy new land and split their communities. This had the additional benefit of keeping communities to a size that allowed face-to-face communication and intimate personal contacts between all members. This in turn restrained the growth of formal structures of leadership and thus prevented Michels' oligarchy.

The point is that bromides always do what bromides do. People can think about what they do. This does not mean they can always master themselves or their circumstances, but it does mean that they can learn from their mistakes and from others. And they can learn from sociology. People who wish to start a commune can now read and learn from Kanter's studies. Leaders of left-wing parties can study Michels and do their best to avoid the pitfalls of oligarchy.

However, the Burns problem will always beset human action. If we wish to understand what people are doing and why, we must be interested in their motives and intentions, in how they see the world. But if we wish to understand why the world is as it is, we need to be concerned with unintended and unanticipated consequences.

# Chapter 4
# The modern world

## The observer and the observed

Sociology has an unusual relationship with its subject matter. Although we can view it as a disinterested intellectual discipline that stands aside from the world it observes, sociology is itself a symptom of the very things it describes.

In his work on Puritans in science, Robert Merton argued that the religion of the Jews and then Christianity were rationalizing forces. By having just one God instead of a pantheon of deities (who often operated erratically and at cross purposes), and by confining God to creating and ending the world but not interfering much in between, Christianity permitted a scientific attitude to the material world because it assumed that the world was orderly. Furthermore, the material world was not itself sacred in any sense that inhibited its systematic study. Once the Reformation had rejected the authority of the Roman Church, scientists were free to pursue their scholarship unhindered by religious imperatives. According to Merton, what made modern science possible was not technical advances in instrumentation (though those were important) so much as a new way of looking at the world.

A similar case can be made for why sociology appears when it does. The 14th-century Arab philosopher Ibn Khaldun or the ancient

Greeks Plato and Aristotle made sociological observations in the course of their philosophical and historical writings, but it is not until Adam Smith, David Hume, and Adam Ferguson at the end of the 18th century that we find, in the Scottish Enlightenment, a body of academic work that would be recognizable to modern sociologists, and it is not until the 20th century that the discipline flourished. This is not an accident. In a traditional society with a coherent and all-embracing culture, few-but-powerful social institutions, and an all-pervasive religion that bolsters those institutions with divine authority, it is not easy to see the world as socially constructed. Though some people knew that things could be different and had even have travelled to foreign countries with very different cultures, the solidity of their own taken-for-granted social world repressed the relativizing impact of such knowledge. The weakening of traditions, the decline of religious legitimations for the social order, and increasing social diversity were all necessary preconditions for sociology.

## Modernity

This seems a good point to spell out in some detail the distinctive features of modern times. By 'modern' I do not mean 'extant now'; the term implies more than chronology. Modernization refers to a series of long-run and complex consequences of changes in the ratio of inanimate to animate power. Unless Von Däniken was right about alien spacemen, the ancient Egyptian pyramids were built by men and beasts with only levers and inclined planes to lighten the burden. We build with machines driven by fossil fuels, which massively increases our productive capacity. This account of what follows from that can be no more than a sketch, but it will summarize what sociology sees as distinctive about the social formations that concern it (in contrast to the traditional societies that are studied by anthropologists).

Manufacturing work has become ever more finely divided. Tasks, and the people who perform them, have become so specialized that we are now reliant on each other. Peasants of the Middle Ages owned little they could not make themselves and the possessions of even the rich were produced by only a small number of tradesmen. Now even the poor of Japan or Germany will own goods made on the other side of the world and eat food shipped from another continent. Production has ceased to be a personal activity involving the family and the community. Exchange is conducted through the impersonal medium of cash (rather than barter) and mediated by markets. Although people in industrial societies are far less self-reliant than their agricultural forebears, their helplessness does not strengthen personal bonds. It just increases the need for formal means of coordination. Instead of finding what we need through informal conversations on the village green, we use internet search engines and online directories.

The ever-finer division of labour in production is mirrored in the non-economic sphere as social institutions become increasingly specialized. Industrial societies are far more 'differentiated' than agrarian ones. A good example is the decline in remit of religious institutions. In Europe in the Middle Ages, the Christian Church provided not only access to supernatural power but also civil administration, education, poor relief, and social discipline. Now civil administration is the province of government departments, education is provided by nurseries, schools, and universities, welfare is provided by social-work agencies, and social control is managed by police forces, courts, and prisons.

The family also became more specialized. In agrarian societies, it was usually a unit of production as well as the social institution which managed biological and social reproduction. In industrial societies, most economic activity is conducted in distinct settings with their own values and operating procedures; we leave home to go to work.

The rise of industrialization changed the nature and social consequences of inequality. In theory people became more alike and in many ways the world became fairer. At the same time the social distance between different sorts of people increased. Agrarian societies had considerable disparities of status, but most people lived similar lives and lived cheek-by-jowl. In medieval tower houses and castles, the gentry and their servants often slept in the same room, separated only by curtains. The lord might have clean straw but both lords and servants slept on straw. They ate at the same table, with the salt dish marking off the gentry from the riff-raff. Because the social structure was openly hierarchical, superiors did not feel threatened by the close proximity of their minions and could comfortably inhabit the same physical and mental space. At the same table, the master's family ate meat while his servants ate bread.

Industrialization destroyed the great pyramid of feudal social order. Innovation and economic expansion brought with them occupational mobility. People no longer did the job they had always done because their family had always done that job. Occupational change and social advancement made it hard for people to think of themselves as having a fixed 'station' in life. Furthermore, economic growth brought increased *physical* mobility and greater contact with strangers. Profound inequalities are only tolerable and harmonious if, as in the Hindu caste system, the ranking is widely known and accepted. Soldiers can move from one regiment to another and still know their place because there is a uniform (in both senses) ranking system. In a complex and mobile society, it is not easy to know whether we are superior or subordinate to any stranger. Once people have trouble knowing who should salute first, they stop saluting. Basic equality becomes the norm and the most obvious forms of deference fall out of use.

The egalitarian dynamic is reinforced by the separation of home and work. One cannot be a serf from sunrise to sunset and a free individual for the evening and at weekends. A real serf has to be full time. A lead miner in Rosedale, Yorkshire, in 1800 might be sorely oppressed at work, but in the late evening and on Sunday he could change his clothes and his persona to become a Methodist lay preacher, a person of high prestige and standing. The possibility of such alternation marks a crucial change. Once occupation became freed from an entire all-embracing hierarchy and became task specific, it was possible for people to occupy different positions in different hierarchies. That made it possible to distinguish between the role and the person who played it. Roles could still be ranked and accorded very different degrees of respect, power, or status, but the people who played the roles could be regarded as being in some abstract sense equal. To put it the other way round, so long as people were seen in terms of just one identity in one hierarchy, egalitarianism was impossible because treating alike a peasant and his feudal superior threatened to turn the world upside down.

But once an occupation could be judged apart from the person who performed it, it became possible to maintain a necessary order in the factory, for example, while operating a different system of judgements outside the work context. The ironmaster could rule his workforce but sit alongside his foreman as an elder in the local church. Of course, power and status are often transferable. Being a force in one sphere increases the chances of influence in another. The ironmaster could expect to dominate the congregation of the chapel he paid to have built, but he would do so only if his wealth was matched by manifest piety. If not, his fellow churchgoers could respond to any attempt to impose his will by defecting to a neighbouring congregation. In a nutshell, the fragmentation of the simple traditional society allowed the rise of autonomous individuals who were seen as being, at least in the abstract, much of a muchness.

The structural causes of egalitarianism reinforced, and were reinforced by, ideological pressures in the same direction. It is no coincidence that the first modern industrial societies were predominantly Protestant. The 16th-century Reformation contained within it the seeds of the 'Liberty, Equality, Fraternity' that was preached by the French Revolution more than 200 years later. Martin Luther and John Calvin were not liberals in the modern sense. They held that all people were alike, but only in their sinfulness and before God. Nonetheless, equality in the eyes of God laid the foundations for equality in the eyes of man and before the law. So long as society, polity, and economy were part of a single unified and coherent universe, the inherent egalitarianism of the Reformation was compromised by the insistence of the powerful on maintaining the hierarchy, but, once that single universe had been broken into distinct sectors, the democratic potential could be realized.

The rise of democracy was inadvertently encouraged by one consequence of the Reformation that was coincidentally also a necessary condition for a modern economy and a modern nation-state: the spread of literacy. A religion that requires obedience to the priest class and ritual performance does not need its people to be docile and passive, but it does not promote the alternative. A religion that says everyone must study the Word of God and take personal responsibility for obeying God's commands encourages personal autonomy and needs to provide people with the ability to read the Word. The Reformers translated the Bible from Latin, the international language of the educated, into the many languages of the common people. And they taught the masses to read. The revolutionary potential of that was well understood. As late as the start of the 19th century Hannah More, an evangelical Christian who created a string of schools in the Mendips, tried to teach her pupils only to read, not to write. Writing was dangerously liberating, but reading, especially reading the socially conservative and morally uplifting tracts she produced, was safe. She failed. Her pupils took their new skills and turned them to their own needs.

The point about egalitarianism is often misunderstood. I am not suggesting that modernization swept away differences of wealth and power. I am saying, with Marx, that the class structure of industrial capitalism was simpler and more fluid than the hierarchies it superseded because it replaced the complex web of feudal obligations and reciprocal responsibilities with the simple contract. And, because people no longer felt comfortable admitting them, differences of wealth, power, and status were more often disguised.

Where Marx was wrong was in his belief that classes would become ever more rigid as all other social divisions became replaced by what he called 'relationship to the means of production'. In Marx's vision there would be just two great classes: the capitalist, who owned the means of production, and the proletarians, who did not. Increasing conflict between these two blocs would eventually lead to the final revolution when private property would be swept away and communism would replace capitalism.

Clearly Marx was wrong about the revolution, and that error stemmed from his mistake about the increasing rigidity of class divisions. Far from becoming ever more sclerotic, class divisions softened. As Weber pointed out, there were major divisions within Marx's classes. In Marxist theory, all proletarians were in the same (ever more leaky) boat, but, as Weber correctly saw, those who were alike in lacking productive capital could still differ in power and hence in life chances. Those whose skills were scarce (professional workers, for example) could exert considerable command over their working conditions and pay. There was also an important group of managers who, although lacking capital, nonetheless, through their day-to-day control of capitalist enterprises, enjoyed a position quite different from that of unskilled workers. Furthermore, the rise of the joint stock company meant that an increasing amount of capital was owned, not by individuals but by collective agents such as pension funds and insurance companies.

Marx also failed to appreciate the consequence of *flow* within occupational structures. Through the 19th and early 20th centuries, the proportion of people who worked in agriculture steadily fell: farm labourers moved into the towns and cities and into the factories. In the 20th century the proportion of people who worked at unskilled manual jobs fell steadily. In 1911 over three-quarters of Britain's employed were manual workers. By 1964 this had fallen to half and by 1987 it was only a third. Even if we can view the class structure as a stable pyramid of boxes (and more of that shortly), the content of those boxes has been in constant flux. People have moved in and out of them, often in only one generation, almost always in two. This offers one very powerful reason why people did not, as Marx expected, come to see themselves as being much defined by their class: they were not in any one social place long enough.

Weber's way of conceptualizing class as a market situation, and its focus on structured differences in rewards and autonomy, has proved more fruitful than Marx's capital-and-labour schema. Class analysis now commonly divides people as follows. Those in the service class or *salariat* exercise delegated authority or specialized knowledge and expertise on behalf of their employing organization. In return, they enjoy decent incomes, job security, incremental advances, pension rights, and a good deal of freedom to shape their work as they see fit. The *working class* consists of skilled and unskilled manual workers who supply discrete amounts of labour in a relatively short-term and specific exchange of effort for money. These occupations are more intensively supervised and controlled.

Between the service class and the working class, we have the *routine clerical* class, which is defined by employment relations that combine elements of the service relationship and the pure labour contract. A fourth class consists of the *small proprietors and self-employed*, who enjoy the autonomy of the service class but also exchange effort for money on a 'piece' or time basis. Finally, we distinguish *farmers* and *agricultural workers*, whose working lives often differ markedly from those of other kinds of small proprietors and manual workers: they own land, involve their families in production, and offer and receive payment in kind (such as tied housing).

Although these divisions are more complex than what we commonsensically mean by class, this system has a number of advantages. First, the categories are based on a clear and testable theory about what matters for life chances. Second, they have repeatedly been shown to be effective in explaining social regularities. Third, they have been extensively used in cross-national comparisons of social mobility.

By social mobility we mean the extent of movement between classes and we usually have two questions in mind. How likely is it that someone will move from one class to another in his or her lifetime? How likely is it that people will end up in a class that is not the same as that of their parents? One of the most surprising results of modern class analysis is that the relative chances of changing position vary little from one society to another. We may suppose that such new or radically restructured societies as Japan, Australia, and the United States are much more open than Britain, but reliable studies have shown that these and other major industrial societies have very similar mobility regimes; that is, that they are similarly fluid. Furthermore, though those of us lucky enough to have benefited from the change in the class structure might find this hard to believe, relative class mobility chances remained much the same during the 20th century.

This finding surprises us because we tend to think of life chances as properties of individuals rather than as features of social structures. Social mobility is a product not just of the characteristics of mobile individuals but also of the capacity of places of origin and destination. Whatever class you are born in, the odds of improving yourself depend not just on the fluidity of the system but also on the size of the box you want to end up in. Over the 20th century the shape of the class hierarchy changed from a pyramid (with a small elite, a slightly larger service class, and a large working class) to a lozenge, as the number of people involved in manual work declined and the white-collar and professional sectors grew rapidly. As a result of that change, everyone had a better chance of moving up, but the *relative* chances of someone from the bottom of the pile and someone from the top ending up at the top, remained much the same. As Gordon Marshall put it:

> More 'room at the top' has not been accompanied by greater equality in the opportunities to get there. All that has happened is that proportionately more of the new salariat jobs have gone to the children of parents already holding privileged class locations. In sum the growth of skilled white-collar work has increased opportunities for mobility generally, but the distribution of those opportunities across the class has stayed the same.

In other words, children of the working class benefited from the expansion of white-collar work, but then so did the children of the middle classes.

What we make of this depends largely on what we want or expect. If we are interested in social justice, we might find it rather depressing that those at the top retained their advantages. However, if we are interested in *absolute* social mobility, then we would still be impressed that so many working-class people rose into the service class, even though there was not a corresponding number of service-class people going the other way. That lots of people now have more comfortable and affluent lives owes far more to changes in the economy than to greater equality of opportunity, but that should not blind us to the scale of the change.

The expansion of the service class can serve as a link to the next element in my description of modernization: the rise of the nation-state. We are so used to maps that divide the world into France, Germany, Italy, and the like, and to wars between nations, that we can easily miss the novelty of this way of dividing and organizing people. Ethnic groups, united among themselves and divided from their neighbours by religion and language, are ancient, but until the 18th century most economies and polities were either larger or smaller than the present nation: villages and towns for some things; monarchies (which might encompass lands in a number of countries) and empires for others. The rise of the nation-state brought with it the need for ever-increasing numbers of officials to staff its machinery of government. In the 20th century the nation-state became the welfare state, and that created a vast array of professional middle-class jobs in health, social security, housing, and education.

That modern lives are organized more by nation-states than by communities has paradoxical consequences for the links between society and culture. On the one hand, the nation-state requires a certain degree of internal homogeneity and promotes a sense of shared identity through a common language and a national (preferably heroic) history. It demands loyalty to the fatherland or motherland. But, at the same time, the modern nation-state has to come to terms with considerable cultural diversity within its borders.

Diversity comes from various sources. People migrate and take their culture with them; this has been the experience of New World states such as the United States, Canada, or Australia. The state may expand to encompass new peoples, as happened when Britain expanded to become the United Kingdom. Unitary states may be created from a number of republics, kingdoms, and principalities, as with Germany and Italy. But modernization itself creates cultural diversity *within* a society. In the feudal world a single church encompassed almost the entire population and imposed something like a unitary set of values and norms on the people. With industrialization, communities of like-situated people fragmented into classes that developed their own interests. That increasing social diversity was reflected in the religious culture, which, if it was Protestant, fragmented into competing religious organizations or, if it was Catholic or Lutheran, divided more radically into the enduringly religious and the liberal secular. The gentry (and the agricultural labourers they controlled) stayed with the national church; its hierarchical structure of archbishops, bishops, and priests suited well the aristocratic view of the world as a divinely ordained pyramid. But the urban merchants, skilled craftsmen, and the more independent farmers were drawn to more democratic forms of religion and supported a series of schisms. The details of the break-up of what was once a unified culture are less important than the consequence.

Faced with growing social diversity, the state had a simple choice. It could try to coerce conformity or it could become tolerant. Usually toleration was the second preference, accepted only when trying to coerce conformity patently failed, and accepted only recently. In Britain, it was not until the middle of the 19th century that the final restrictions on religious dissenters were removed. Catholics did not get the vote until 1829. Oxford and Cambridge had religious tests for entry until the 1870s and it was not until 1891 that such tests for Members of Parliament were abolished. These were the last vestiges of attempts to preserve a national religious culture that had looked pretty shaky since the 18th century. Despite persecution, the Quakers became wealthy and powerful, and by the 1830s the Methodists and Baptists were too numerous to be excluded from public life. Increasing diversity, combined with the already described rise of egalitarianism, forced the state to accept cultural differences. In the leading modern countries, ethnic nationalism (which supposes that national belonging requires cultural cohesion and common ancestry) was mostly replaced by a civic nationalism which requires only that citizens obey the law, pay their taxes, and, if required, fight to defend the nation.

Long term, cultural pluralism brought about fundamental changes in the structure of social life and in its psychology. At the societal level, we see an increasing division between the public and the private world. People became increasingly free to do what they liked at home, at leisure, in private. At the same time, toleration was increasingly enforced by procedural rules in the public sphere. Many illustrations of this momentous change can be seen in how we use the term 'discrimination'. In the early 19th century it was quite normal for someone who held a powerful public office to use it to promote the interests of his family and friends. Patronage was the key to social advancement. Large landowners who controlled church appointments, for example, were expected to give rich parishes or posts on the staff of cathedrals to their kinsmen or to the sons of other wealthy patrons who could return the favour. Senior army officers and civil servants would appoint their relatives to offices they controlled. We would now regard such a system as unfair. Nepotism (that is, advancing the interests of one's kin) is no longer a descriptive term; it is an accusation. More than that—and this offers another important insight into the logic of the modern world—we would regard such a system as inefficient.

Modern societies take the principles that underlie the industrialization of manufacture and apply them to the organization of people in other spheres. We suppose that any task is best done if we concentrate on the matter in hand and disregard other considerations. We expect soldiers to be promoted if they show an aptitude for soldiering and not because they are the sons of generals. We expect clergy will be appointed because they show appropriate spirituality and not because their families have some pull with the gentry of the parish. Admission to higher education is by academic qualifications. Concentration on the task in hand requires us to be 'universalistic'. For example, we suppose that the most efficient and fairest way of allocating publically owned social housing is to establish criteria of need (such as number of children and state of present housing) and allocate houses as they become vacant to those with the greatest need. If we discover that elected councillors are representing their more bigoted constituents by denying council houses to poor immigrants, we accuse them of discrimination and we create new sets of rules and procedures to put housing allocation on a rational and fair basis.

Of course, powerful groups do not readily bow to the demands for civil rights and in many arenas we see lengthy cat-and-mouse games. When the United States gave the vote to black people, many southern states tried to preserve white supremacy by creating requirements of voters (such as literacy tests) that superficially looked fair, in that they applied to everyone, but were actually intended to curb black voting. When, despite this, black people began to vote in large numbers, electoral districts were drawn up in ways that reduced the effectiveness of their vote. By creating a large number of low-density white congressional districts and a small number of districts that encompassed very large numbers of blacks, one white vote could be made as influential as three or four black votes. The response of the federal government and the courts was to promote new laws that prevented each new evading tactic.

The progress of civil rights in modern societies has been uneven and halting. For all our legislative efforts on equal opportunities, it remains the case that many groups are systematically disadvantaged. While we have a good record of promoting *individual* legal and political rights, and of trying to prevent discrimination, we have done less to redress the considerable disparities of power and wealth that flow from social characteristics such as class, gender, and race. Strategies for redistributing wealth or creating real equality of opportunity by giving disadvantaged groups various sorts of head start have usually been defeated by the counter-argument that they infringe the individual rights of those who cannot claim membership of the group that is intended to benefit from such affirmative action.

The start of the 21st century even saw some progressive trends reversed. Middle-class people became more likely to marry others of the same status and thus more likely to pass their advantages to their children. And even among the working classes, taxing inherited wealth became less popular. In 1917 death duties formed 10 per cent of the UK government's revenues. In 2016 they were less than 1 per cent. A similar pattern can be seen in most modern societies: in the 21st century Sweden entirely abolished inheritance tax. The net result is that wealth is once again becoming concentrated in the hands of the few.

Nonetheless, that our societies retain certain forms of inequality should not blind us to the extent to which they have abandoned others. Modern societies regard as unjust and inefficient, and seek strenuously to outlaw, discriminatory practices that were entirely acceptable 200 years ago. In the 19th century people talked openly about 'knowing your station in life' and 'not getting ideas above your station'; in the 21st century we are coy about class divisions.

To recap, on the one hand, we have the public sphere becoming increasingly free of cultural norms such as 'promote your kin'. On the other hand, we have ever-greater freedom for people to exercise their personal preferences. Religious preferences and sexual orientation are now largely matters for individuals. The important point the sociologist would make about these changes, which separates the sociological explanation from that of the idealist philosopher, is that increasing personal freedom and liberty did not come about because any particular person or group thought liberty was a good idea. It was not the sloganeering of the French revolutionaries or black civil-rights activists that made the world as it is. Such social movements largely legitimated and reinforced changes that were already underway as a necessary accommodation to the forces of modernization. Changes in the economic and political structure required changes in our basic attitudes to people. The division of public from private was a necessary accommodation to increasing social and cultural diversity in a context that assumes all people are at base equal and is unwilling to pay the price of enduring conflict.

That describes the structural response to social fragmentation. There was also a powerful change in the way we hold our beliefs and values. We saw it first in religion, but it spread. When the dominant religious cultures first fragmented, each fraction insisted that it and only it was right, but with increased diversity such conviction became fragile. One good way to sustain it is to devise a theory which both asserts the superiority of one's own views and explains why other people have got it wrong. The British missionaries of the 19th century argued that God revealed himself in forms appropriate to the social evolution of different races. To the aborigines and Africans he gave animism. The more developed Arabs got Islam. The southern Europeans got Catholic Christianity. But to the northern Europeans (and especially the British) he revealed himself fully in evangelical Protestantism. We can appreciate the value of this argument for those who promoted it. It prevented them taking alternatives seriously; it explained why others were wrong without accusing them of malevolence; it asserted the primacy of British Protestantism; and it justified British imperialism. By 'bringing on' the supposedly backward races the British would raise them to the point where they were ready for the true religion.

Another way of protecting one's beliefs from the challenge of alternatives is to suppose that those who disagree with us are in thrall to some evil power. So American fundamentalists of the Cold War era supposed that liberal Christians were either in the pay or the power of Soviet Communism. All such strategies work best when the dissenters are arguably alien, not our sort of people, which is why the cultural diversity that results from the internal fragmentation of society is more threatening than that which comes from outside. When our own people—our neighbours, friends, and relatives—disagree with us, it is less easy to dismiss them as being of no account. In that situation we are more likely to lower the status and shrink the reach we accord our views. Of course, dogmatism is still common, but, especially as they are expressed in such public forums as the mass media, alternative ideas and beliefs are now often handled in a manner that is in effect relativistic. We manage our failure to agree by supposing that what works for you may not work for me, and vice versa. Truth becomes personalized.

More will be said about relativism in Chapter 5. Here I will summarize by saying that the rise of egalitarian individualism has consequences both for the organization of society (in essence, increased freedom in private and increased constraint in public) and for the status we accord our ideas and values.

## Anomie and social order

This is a slightly contrived link, but I would like to return to the nature of social order and the causes of crime, and the topic of egalitarianism does feature in what follows. Consider India. It is a country with extremes of wealth and poverty yet, compared to the USA, it has relatively little crime and fewer of the vices we associate with urban social malaise: alcoholism, drug addiction, and suicide. The core explanation is simple and was given in the 1950s by Robert Merton, who took Durkheim's arguments about the link between individual stability and social order and added a radical twist. It is often supposed that the crucial tension in social life is between the individual and the society. Social ill-ease results from a society insufficiently imposing its values on its members; anti-social behaviour comes from a lack of socialization. Merton took the rather different view that a tendency to crime and deviance was actually endemic to the modern society.

This summary simplifies, but Merton's case was that societies have two relatively autonomous spheres: culture and social structure. Culture tells us two sorts of things: what we should desire and how we should behave. Structure allocates power, wealth, and status. The social structures of traditional societies are hierarchical. Some people are rich and powerful; most are impotent and poor, and the culture justifies that disparity. Different classes of people are taught to expect very different things from life and to behave in ways appropriate to their station. Hence what people expect and what they get are balanced. Because the poor expect to be poor, they accept their poverty. In medieval Europe and in Hindu India this profoundly discriminatory system was legitimated by a widely shared religion that promised rewards in the next life to those who humbly accepted their lack of them in this life. The meek Christian will inherit the earth in the next life provided he does not try to steal it in this and the poor but pious Hindu will be rewarded with a better rebirth.

What puts conflict at the heart of the modern social system is that culture and social structure are no longer in harmony. The culture is democratic: the goals of material success are offered equally to everyone. The American dream promises that anyone can become President of the United States or at least president of a major corporation. Merton quotes the industrialist Andrew Carnegie: 'Be a king in your dreams. Say to yourself, "My place is at the top".' He goes further and suggests that the United States (and here it may differ in degree from many European societies) makes ambition patriotic.

But equality of aspiration is not matched by equality of opportunity. The rhetoric of meritocracy encourages everyone to want the same things, but the reality of class structure means many people cannot attain their goals legitimately. As the social structure does not let them remain equally committed to the socially approved goals and to the socially approved means, they must abandon one (or both) parts of the value system. Logically there are five ways people may adapt to this tension.

To the extent that a society is stable, then conformity will be the most common and widely diffused position. Most people are committed to the goals and to the rules that specify how one attains them. That is, they want to get on and accept the goals of fame and fortune but wish to achieve those ends only by socially acceptable means.

In contrast, Merton's second type—the innovators—are committed to the end result but reject the procedural rules. The combination of relentless emphasis on success with the uneven distribution of legitimate means to achieve it allows many people to feel justified in finding new (and illegal) ways to become successful. Denied any real hope of becoming rich legitimately, the ambitious poor may seek fame and fortune through crime.

The third type of adaptation, ritualism, is less obvious but nonetheless interesting. British social history offers many studies of the almost obsessively respectable lower-middle class and the type is well explored in the early novels of George Orwell. Here are people who have no serious prospect of being successful but who are terrified of being mistaken for, or worse, actually falling into, the rough working class they have learnt to despise. Dress, demeanour, and language codes all become important devices for drawing a clear line between the respectable and the rough. Ritualism is the perspective of the zealously conformist bureaucrat whose sense of self-worth is derived from shallow similarities to the class above and deep disdain for the one below.

The retreatist response is the least common. In this category fall some of the adaptive activities of 'psychotics, autists, pariahs, outcasts, vagrants, vagabonds, tramps, chronic drunkards and drug addicts': people who have given up on goals and means and, indeed, on most of life above the biological.

Merton's first four responses to the tension between ends and means are the logical combinations of being 'on' or 'off' on the two principles: +/+, +/−, −/+, and −/−. But it is obviously possible for people to be selective (that is, a bit of + and a bit of −) on either principle. Hence he adds the fifth category of rebellion to describe the deliberately selective attitude to goals and means of those people who seek to replace the prevailing order by a new improved world in which merit, effort, and reward are brought into alignment.

As with many other sociological classics, Merton's theory of anomie inspired a large body of research that confirmed some elements of the model and cast doubt on others. In particular, scholars were critical of Merton's view that innovation is most strongly associated with the blocked working class. That disillusionment with the unfairness of a class society causes the disadvantaged to seek to enrich themselves by robbery, burglary, theft, and mugging seems plausible, but why do some of those who have every opportunity to do well honestly nonetheless want to do better dishonestly? Why do wealthy financiers fiddle their customers? Why do rich businessmen cheat their taxes? Why does an already prosperous pharmaceutical company illegally defraud its customers by reducing the dosage of its pre-filled syringes while leaving the price the same? Although Merton does discuss white-collar crime, his view from the 1950s now seems rather naïve. As journalists have become less deferential to the rich and powerful, we have learnt a great deal about the workings of power elites and it is now difficult to share Merton's confidence that criminal 'innovation' is especially the preserve of the deprived.

But Merton did capture a vital feature of modern societies. Stable societies rest on a consensus that things are mostly as they *should* be. They do not require the universal and enthusiastic embrace of a single dominant ideology that justifies social arrangements in detail but there does need to be some general sense that people get their just deserts. The Hindu notion of karma achieves that perfectly. Because it is built on the principle of repeated reincarnation, it can suppose that, however unfair things look right now, bad people with good lives must have been better in a previous incarnation and, furthermore, they will suffer a worse rebirth in the next life as punishment for their acts in this round. Though Christianity is less good at explaining why bad things happen to good people, it offers a restorative mechanism in the notions of heaven and hell. But modern societies are largely secular and our desire for social justice has to be satisfied in this material world.

The egalitarian impulse, which, I have argued, is a central feature of the modern world, challenges the manifest inequalities of life. So long as meritocracy remains more an aspiration than a reality, those who are encouraged to want a slice of the action but feel themselves denied a fair break will have little compunction about taking what is due to them. The American journalist, Studs Terkel, once suggested that the motto of Chicago should be the frankly acquisitive 'Where's mine?' Mass communication plays an important role in stimulating demand universally: television ads for fast cars do not carry a health warning saying 'By the way, most of you should not covet this because you will never be able to afford it.'

Merton's theory may be saved from the problem of the prosperous law-breaker (though much diluted by this rewriting) by returning to Durkheim's argument about the boundless nature of human desires. Someone who has everything can still want more, and a culture that puts great stress on worldly success while promoting the rights of the individual over the interests of the community encourages everyone, irrespective of their objective position, to feel relatively deprived.

## Postmodernity?

Although scholars differ in the weight they give to different causes in this account of modernization, it is widely agreed that industrial societies are fundamentally unlike their agrarian predecessors. For most of the 20th century, there was an argument about which features of modernity were a consequence of industrialization as such and which followed from the capitalist economy in which our industrialization had taken shape. The class structures, gender relations, patterns of religious observation, and crime rates of capitalist democracies were compared with those of eastern European states of the communist bloc. The collapse of communism in the 1980s ended those debates. The attempt to see which parts of our past were somehow inevitable and which accidental has now shifted to comparison of the past of the West (or First World) and the present of countries in the Global South (or Third World). It is, for example, now possible to understand better our own history when we see how the development of the nation-state, representative politics, and industrialization proceed in the very different context of Singapore, Japan, the two Koreas, and China. If nothing else, the existence of such comparators has undermined confidence in the 1950s sociology that saw the history of the West as providing a universal template for modernization.

One reason the history of the West cannot simply repeat is that, when it modernized, it innovated without known destinations or maps to guide the journey. There were no existing models. Modernity now exists and for some societies (Kemal Atatürk's Turkey in the 1920s and 1930s, for example) it serves as model for emulation while for others (contemporary Muslim fundamentalists, for example) it represents a 'great Satan' to be repudiated and attacked. Even when Western powers do not interfere militarily in most corners of the globe, they sell and buy goods and services internationally and mass communication means that the culture and mores of the West can only be ignored with the sort of repressive efforts expended by North Korea.

Since the last decades of the 20th century there has been an important shift in depictions of the West as many scholars (interestingly often philosophers and social theorists rather than sociologists) have argued that, though the account of modernization in this chapter is reasonably accurate for the 19th and early 20th centuries, we have now moved into another epoch: the *postmodern* world. Although there are many strands to postmodernism (which was an art style before it became a social theory), the basic idea is that individual freedom has combined with increased geographical mobility and better communication to create a world in which 'consumers' select elements of culture from a global cafeteria. Economies based on the production and distribution of things have been superseded by economies based on the production and distribution of ideas and images. Idiosyncratic preference, taste, and choice have extended to the degree that it makes little sense to talk of social formations such as social class as constraining objective or intersubjective realities.

An obvious illustration can be found in the matter of accents. Before the 1970s there was a clear association between speech styles and social prestige. British news announcers sounded like Queen Elizabeth. One could guess the political party of a politician by accent. British Conservatives spoke like the gentry; Labour politicians spoke in the regional tones of the working class. Such typing is now vastly more difficult. Well-educated middle-class children borrow vocabulary from 'the street' and over her lifetime Queen Elizabeth's accent shifted down a class.

Although there are distinct luxury brands, the proliferation of consumer goods and the decline in their relative cost has permitted an apparent softening of class divisions. Almost everyone in the West has a mobile phone and dresses in similar styles. Cars are ubiquitous and flying and foreign holidays are now commonplace.

In politics, it is no longer simple to infer people's political preferences from their position in the class structure. This is not just a matter of previous deviations (such as the deferential manual worker who voted Conservative) becoming common enough to reverse previous alignments. That has indeed happened in places: the typical member of the British Labour Party is now a middle-class professional rather than a unionized manual worker, and large parts of the American working class and poor now vote Republican. But postmodernity postulates two supposedly novel developments: the declining importance of economic interests and the growing importance of individual preference and identification.

The first can be seen in a variety of consciously created interest groups: radical student movements, environmental movements, animal rights campaigns, gay rights groups, and women's groups. The second can be seen in the 21st century's apparent acceptance (at least in certain class fractions) of social identity as a matter of personal choice. In the more metropolitan parts of modern societies it is increasingly common for people to claim to 'identify as' black, or American Indian, or male or female. Such identification may be claimed irrespective of objective reality but also irrespective of the part that groups traditionally play in deciding who belongs to them. So some people who were born biologically male identify as female without reference to any right of women-who-were-born-women to decide whether such claims are legitimate. Personal preference is treated by some as a card that trumps objective and intersubjective realities.

The postmodern depiction also supposes that the nation-state has become impotent. The globalization of trade and finance reduces the ability of states to control their economies and impose taxes; digital technologies of communication weaken the ability of states to control the information available to their citizens; supranational entities such as the European Union undermine nation-states.

As the gender transitioning example shows, even the certainties of birth, sex, and death have been blown away by innovations in science and medicine. We have now cloned a sheep. We will soon clone people. In the postmodern world, nothing is solid. All is flux.

While there is something in such a description, it is grossly exaggerated. It is always useful to remind the intellectuals of London, Paris, and New York that much provincial life goes on little changed. Satellites and the internet have given us novel forms of communication, but the soap operas we watch are little different from the novels of Dickens; indeed Victorian fiction still provides much of our digital content. Cheap international travel is now possible, but it takes as long to cross London now as it did when Sherlock Holmes solved the crimes of Victorian London. The heavy industries of the Ruhr and the Clyde have disappeared, but many workers are still organized in trade unions and occupational class still affects people's attitudes, beliefs, and political behaviour. Far from withering, the nation-state remains powerful, and a large part of the population of advanced societies now try to reject the local evidence of globalization by voting for right-wing religio-ethnic movements. When states fall apart it is not usually because national identity has weakened; it is because religio-ethnic minorities want their own state.

More significantly for the postmodern image of autonomous actors who express their identities through consumer preferences, the two most obdurate realities of most people's lives—their health and their lifespan—remain heavily determined by class. At the start of the 20th century, working-class boys in London and Glasgow were on average 2.5 inches shorter than their middle-class counterparts. At the end of the century, though everyone had grown, that difference remained. In the 19th century poor people were thin and rich people fat. Now the rich are stick-thin and exercise while the poor are obese and sedentary. The precise relationship between wealth and body mass has flipped over but there is still a vital and debilitating difference. In 2017 the death rate for the once-industrial city of Glasgow, home to some of Britain's poorest people, was twice that of the London borough of Kensington and Chelsea. Life expectancy in the English town of Blackpool was only 74.3, which was five years less than the national average. The proximate explanation can be seen in the fact that Blackpool was also in first or second place for alcoholism, liver disease, and smoking; the deep background explanation is poverty.

The social structures of emotional life have indeed become more complex. Homosexuality is now widely accepted. Gay marriage, divorce, the marriages of adults with children, and the increased longevity that makes three-generation households more common have all made the family a more complex institution than it was in the 19th century, but it remains the primary unit of reproduction and socialization and, for most of us, it remains a desired source of great satisfaction and psychic stability. Cheap high-speed travel allows us to be further away from each other, but it also allows us to regroup frequently.

It may well be that the modern societies which preoccupied and shaped sociology in its first century were so dependent for their character on industrial manufacturing that a shift to an economy based on technological expertise and exchange will cause such far-reaching changes to society and culture that we will, by the middle of the 21st century, be justified in claiming a new epoch. But at present such a designation seems premature.

## Ironic consequences and social policy

To avoid repetition, one consequence of the ironic nature of social action has been held over to this point. The key sociological proposition that much of our world is inadvertent and unintended is important, not just for understanding why things do not go as planned, but also for understanding why things are as they are. This has serious policy implications, because, if we misunderstand the causes of what concerns us, we misdirect our efforts to change it.

The point can be illustrated by considering the conservative critique of modern sexual liberality. Those who bemoan the decline of the traditional family often blame the proportion of children in day care, juvenile pregnancies, high divorce rates, and, by extension, urban crime and juvenile delinquency, on individuals or social-movement organizations that openly championed contraception, sexual liberation, easier divorce, and alternatives to the monogamous lifelong heterosexual nuclear family. Liberal writers from the 'Permissive Society' of the 1960s or supporters of gay marriages from the 2000s are quoted and their opinions are taken to have been effective. That is, the problems were caused by these bad people. Hence the solution is for liberals to be restrained and conservatives to be encouraged.

However, a sociological approach to increasing divorce rates would suggest that, far from being the deliberate outcome of consciously desired ends, they are the *unintended consequences* of interacting developments, many of them supported by and enjoyed by the conservatives who bemoan the consequences. Much of the previous stability of marriage came from its role in allocating property and determining inheritance. When resources were largely heritable capital, determining who was a legitimate heir was a vital matter. But industrialization ended the importance of the household as a unit of production and reduced the significance of the difference between legitimate and illegitimate offspring. That change combined with the availability of safe and effective contraception to break the link between sexual fulfilment and reproduction. Industrialization and prosperity reduced the value of large families. Fewer (but better cared for) children meant greater opportunities for women to seek fulfilment and financial independence through work outside the home. When there was a clear gender division of roles, women had little choice but to subordinate personal fulfilment to the stability of the family unit. Increasing individual affluence (and, for those who did not personally prosper, the creation of a welfare state) made people less reliant on their kin and thus made it easier to dissolve unhappy marriages.

The family's loss of economic and political functions allowed space for a new justification: the production of emotional satisfaction. In the 1950s American sociologists such as Talcott Parsons argued that the point of the modern family was to provide psychological comfort and companionship. It was the place to recharge one's emotional batteries and indulge in the expressive and discriminatory behaviour that was increasingly outlawed in the public sphere. At work we were supposed to be rational and disciplined, to be confined by our roles, and to treat people on the basis of universalistic criteria. But at home we could relax and be ourselves. We could be honest. More than that, we were expected to be honest and open, which called into question the hypocrisy that had allowed our forebears to engage in extramarital affairs while swearing lifelong fidelity. What we can now see is that the expectation of emotional fulfilment is both a great boon and an enormous strain on a social unit.

A further strain results from increasing gender equality. As women's earnings have approached those of their husbands they have come to expect a greater say in family decisions. Negotiation has become ever more important in marriage. To return to Goffman's drama metaphor, spouses used to follow fairly fixed scripts; now they have to improvise. And many of us are not very good at that.

A further cause of an increase in divorce can be found in the increase in life expectancy. In 1900 only 8 per cent of the British population was over 60; in 2000 over 20 per cent managed that. It may seem callous to put it this bluntly, but when premature death no longer brings a convenient end to unhappy relationships, we need an alternative.

The specific causal connections are complex, but the above is enough to assure us that the decline of the traditional nuclear family almost certainly owes very little to the writings of the enemies of the family. Their critiques of lifelong monogamy were celebrations, rather than causes of, complex changes already under way. Alterations in the nature of the family cannot be separated from a raft of other changes, few of which socio-moral conservatives would wish to reverse.

The policy implication is this. Ordinary people generally explain changes by the intentions of those who are held responsible for them. Things happen because some people wanted them to happen and were effective in translating their wishes into results. Sociology reminds us of the enormous complexity of the social constructions that underlie actions, of the importance of social forces beyond our immediate appreciation, and of the importance of unintended consequences.

# Chapter 5
# What sociology is not

The previous chapters have tried to give some idea of the themes of sociology and the distinctive flavour of the sociological vision of the world. To clarify further that vision, this chapter will consider how sociology should differ from related and apparently similar enterprises.

## Improvers and utopians

There is an impression, widespread among its detractors and not unknown within the discipline, that sociology is (or should be) in the business of helping people. This is understandable, but it is mistaken. It is understandable because many of the early contributors to the discipline were moved to study the social world by a wish to alter it. Karl Marx was primarily a revolutionary who wished to see unjust and oppressive capitalism replaced by a more humane economic and political structure. Such founders of the British tradition of empirical social research as Seebohm Rowntree and Charles Booth documented poverty because they hoped to shock governments into doing something about it. Sociology in Britain owed a great deal to the London School of Economics, and the close association of that institution with Sidney and Beatrice Webb (the founders of the Fabian Society and an influence on the early Labour Party) who gave much of its work a clearly reformist tone. Some of the founding faculty of the

University of Chicago's Sociology Department had been raised in Protestant clergy families, and, though far from being Marxists, they would have heartily agreed with Marx that the point of studying the world was to change it.

However, though the discipline owes much to reformers, and many sociologists derive their research interests from their moral and political engagement with the world, sociology must be distinguished from social reform. An academic discipline should be driven by only its concerns and not those of others. For sociologists to collaborate in accumulating a body of knowledge, they need to speak a common language. For example, the comparative class analysis mentioned in Chapter 4 is possible only because scholars in different countries use the same models. Debates (for example, over the relative merits of Marxist and Weberian views of class) can be rationally advanced only if both sides agree to deal from the same pack of cards and play by the same rules. For this reason, only those ideas that are necessary to the task in hand should be allowed to guide our work.

That is easier to say than to ensure. Genetics and Soviet communist philosophy are sufficiently different for us to see their mixing in the dead-end work of Lysenko. But the study of social life and the reform of society share concepts, measures, and theories, and that makes it especially difficult to avoid contamination. Nonetheless, such avoidance has to be our aim. Productive dialogue between sociologists is best served by them making every effort to distinguish between the values necessary to the discipline (such as honesty, clarity, and diligence) and extra-disciplinary concerns that should be laid to one side. Those of us who teach sociology routinely see the difficulty our students have in distinguishing between a social and a sociological problem. When asked to choose a topic for their research projects, students almost invariably focus on something bad about the world. They want to 'do something about' the homeless or alcoholism or domestic violence, and the flaccid verb 'to do' is a clear symptom of the confusion between explaining and rectifying.

One way of clarifying the difference is to describe a sociological study of some feature of the social world that might be widely seen as unacceptable. David Sudnow examined 'plea bargaining' in California's courts in the early 1970s. Some 80 per cent of cases never came to trial because the defendant agreed to plead guilty, which saved the courts a lot of money. To encourage the defendant to 'cop a plea', some reduction in the charge was usually offered. The supposed perpetrator was given a choice between contesting the case and risking a certain level of punishment or accepting as certain a lower level of punishment.

The California legal code recognized the notion of a lesser offence. If in committing crime A, a person must also commit crime B and B gets a shorter custodial sentence, then B is the lesser offence. For example, robbery necessarily included petty theft in the sense that one could not rob without also committing petty theft. Court rules specified that a person could not be charged with two crimes, one of which was necessarily included in the other. For example, a person could not be charged with 'homicide' and with the necessarily included lesser offence of 'intent to commit a murder'. The rules also said that the judge could not instruct a jury to consider, as alternative crimes of which to find the defendant guilty, offences that were not necessarily included in the charged crimes.

Sudnow explains the principles governing lesser offences because he wants to make a contrast between the formal rules and what actually happens. The prosecuting District Attorney and the Public Defender (hereafter DA and PD) had an unusual interest in lesser offences. Rather than being concerned with what crimes were actually committed and the procedural rules about inclusion, they were concerned to strike a bargain. To persuade the defendant to enter a guilty plea, they had to find a lesser offence that carried a sentence sufficiently lower to seem like a good deal but not so much lower that the DA would feel that the defendant had 'got away with it'.

Sudnow discovered that offences were routinely reduced to others that were neither necessarily included nor actually included in the commission of the major offence. For example, 'drunkenness' was often reduced to 'disturbing the peace', even if the peace had not been disturbed. 'Molesting a minor' was often reduced to 'loitering around a schoolyard', even when the offence had taken place nowhere near a schoolyard. Furthermore, reductions often defied the legal definition of the original charge. Burglary was often reduced to petty theft, even though petty theft is necessarily included in robbery and robbery is clearly distinguished in law from burglary. Were one to take the legal code seriously, such a reduction would be a nonsense, yet it was routinely used. Why the DA and PD colluded in this defiance of the law is obvious: all parties had a greater interest in the practical outcome than in the letter of the law.

But how was this practical goal achieved? The answer is that, through lengthy experience, prosecutors and defenders had learnt the typical manner in which offences of given classes were committed, the social characteristics of the people who regularly committed them, the features of the settings in which they occurred, the types of victims usually involved, and the like. They had built up a notion of 'normal crimes'. Over a history of plea bargaining the two sides had developed recipes for successful reductions for what seemed like typical crimes. Typical 'assaults with a deadly weapon' were reduced to simple 'assault', 'molesting' to 'loitering around a schoolyard', and so on. Although the recipes were applied to individual defendants, the particularities of each case were of little concern provided the offence and the offender fitted the typical expectations. It was the class of offence and offender that were at issue and charge sheets were written up in such a way as to steer everyone to the correct interpretation. So the harassed lawyers, who might typically have only a few minutes to review the case, could quickly see what was required and what would work. Only if there was something glaringly unusual about some case would its specific details prompt the 'Hang on. You've missed...' response from defender, prosecutor, or judge that would hold up proceedings.

We could read Sudnow's study as a report on a social problem. The cut-price justice that the system offered could be construed as a major infringement of civil liberties: people routinely pleaded guilty to offences which they had not committed and which nobody thought they had committed. However, none of that is Sudnow's concern. He wants to know not whether the justice routinely doled out by the courts is good or bad, but what it is and how it happens. He is not in the first instance studying a problem to be solved but a thing to be explained. He wants to understand how people in a variety of work settings use ad hoc typifications of their materials to allow them to 'get on with the job' while bypassing, rather than challenging, the formal rhetoric.

A similar theme informed the research of a postgraduate student who was a contemporary of mine in the 1970s. She wanted to understand the practical organization of psychiatric nursing, and for a number of months she worked undercover in a major mental institution. She quickly discovered that patients were managed within two quite different frameworks. The consultant psychiatrists classified patients according to formal diagnostic schema and prescribed treatment appropriate to diagnostic categories. But the nurses, responsible for the day-to-day running of the wards, had a much simpler system that reflected their practical concerns: they labelled patients as 'wetters' and 'wanderers'.

The primary problem with the former was their incontinence; with the latter it was their lack of orientation. The nurses knew their classificatory system would offend the consultants and the family and friends of the patients, so those terms were used only in private talk between nurses and in the 'backstage areas' such as the tea-room, the canteen, and the nurses' home. The police officers who tried to manage the Northern Ireland conflict used a similarly tangential set of labels: for example, a Republican killing of a civilian or a Loyalist paramilitary was 'terrorism', but Republicans killing one of their own members was 'house-keeping', and there was an unstated but clear understanding that some house-keeping would be tolerated so that the organizations could control their wilder elements.

Like Dalton's work on the disjuncture between formal models of organization and the informal organization of the workplace, these examples could be seen as identifying problems, and no doubt particular interest groups will wish to complain about them. But rectifying the world cannot be the sociologists' first concern. In setting their agenda, sociologists must be driven by what is sociologically interesting, not what is socially problematic. Only once they can describe and explain can they take our understanding of some field to the point where sensible policy proposals can be made.

Agendas external to the discipline are an unhelpful distraction. Had Goffman viewed the mental institutions that provided much of the material for *Asylums* from the perspective of either the psychiatrists or their critics, he might have missed the sociological gold dust. Goffman takes a wide variety of trivial and previously unremarked bits of behaviour (such as using crayons as lipstick) and shows that they share a common and important social function: they are devices that patients use to maintain a sense of self-identity in a setting that was designed, for therapeutic purposes, to undermine it. Goffman finds the new meaning in what he observes because he approaches the field as a sociologist. Instead of seeing boarding schools, asylums, monasteries, and army training camps as unrelated places that should be seen as respectively educational, therapeutic, religious, and military, Goffman sees that they have common sociological features that he expresses in the notion of a 'total institution'. Because he was thinking sociologically, Goffman asked questions of his data that others with different agendas and interests would not have considered.

## Partisans

The social sciences are particularly vulnerable to betrayal of principle because a central premise can, if misunderstood, provide a warrant for partisanship. When we recognize that reality is a human product, a social construction, we weaken the solid link between perception and objective reality and call into question the standing of our own accounts and explanations. We then go further and point out that how people see things owes a lot to their shared interests.

This is not a claim about honesty (though it can be closely related); it is about something more subtle than lying. What distinguishes ideology from dissembling is that ideologists believe. When conservative Christians in the United States claim (let us assume mistakenly) that the high level of teenage pregnancy is a result of atheists banning prayer from public schools, they are not lying. They are being influenced by their shared beliefs into seeing the world in a particular way. When entrepreneurs argue that the extension of labour rights will cost jobs, they are not dissembling. They are giving voice to views they sincerely hold, which happily happen to coincide with their material interests.

The natural temptation is to see our own views as accurate and the views of others as ideology, but sociology makes that difficult by identifying ideological influences in an ever-greater number of social groups. Two examples come particularly close to home. In the 1960s it was common to distinguish professions from other kinds of work by noting that doctors and lawyers, for example, experienced lengthy periods of training in which they acquired expertise, were free from external regulation (only a doctor is able to judge if a colleague has been negligent), could restrict entry to the profession, and enjoyed high levels of reward. A firm line was drawn between the professions and other forms of skilled labour (such as craft engineering) that also tried to limit access and thus improve rewards. When the professions did this, it was justified because they served some higher social good (health or justice, for example). When engineers did it, it was an unwarranted restraint on trade, and in many countries it was outlawed.

Sociological studies quickly punctured the inflated self-image of professionals by showing that, although their advantages were real enough, the justifications offered for them were largely self-serving rhetoric. The lengthy training periods often had more to do with excluding those of the wrong class, race, and gender than with the acquiring of necessary skills. Professional self-regulation often had more to do with hiding bad practice from lay scrutiny than with advancing the social good. Professionals seemed as self-interested and acquisitive as any other workers.

The pretensions of science were also deflated by sociological research that showed that scientists were often extremely reluctant to expose their theories to refutation, that the social influence of cliques had a major effect on how new ideas were received, and that there were sometimes no observable differences between the conduct of orthodox and pseudo-science. Far from having a method that guaranteed authority for its results, science looked pretty much like other forms of work. In Chapter 1 I explained why I think this downgrading of science is grossly exaggerated, but it became popular in Western social science.

If sociologists undermine the special status of the professions and the sciences, where does that leave their own work? Does it not follow that the *profession* of social *science* is itself pervaded by ideology? Even if the discipline has no special ideological interests, most of its practitioners would be influenced by the general racial, gender, and class interests of the white, male bourgeoisie.

One seductive resolution to this conundrum is to abandon all pretence of scientific neutrality. As conventional scholarship provides no way of arbitrating between competing visions, we should take sides on grounds derived from outside the discipline and opt for the fully committed partisan vision. Goals such as accuracy are then replaced by an interest in the consequences of ideas: what Karl Marx called *praxis*. What matters is not whether an explanation of crime, for example, is coherent and well supported by the available evidence (because plausibility and evidential status are themselves ideological products), but whether a theory will promote the interests of whatever social group one supports. One brattish criminologist, who himself made no lasting contribution to the subject, preposterously questioned the work of one of the doyens of American criminology by rhetorically asking what Edwin Sutherland had ever done to promote popular struggles!

Another defence for the scholar as partisan has become popular in the areas of ethnic studies and women's studies. The claim here is not that objectivity is impossible; it is that, even if it were possible, it would hinder the sociological enterprise. In order to explain we must understand. In order to understand we must experience. Only a black person can really understand what it means to be black. Only a woman can understand other women.

One good reason to be suspicious of this argument is that it is not offered even-handedly. We do not find sociologists arguing that only aristocrats can usefully study the aristocracy or that only fascists can study fascism. Such special pleading is offered only by people on their own behalf or on behalf of people they like. Often it is simply a way of asserting moral superiority; it is virtue-signalling. Clearly, possessing some trait may be useful in understanding others with the same characteristic. I made that point in my general defence of sociology in Chapter 1. However, there can be no room in honest scholarship for trump cards.

The idea that one has to belong in order to understand is often made further suspect by the way in which the group to which one should belong is defined. In drawing a line between insiders and outsiders, we have to impute to the in-group a patently exaggerated (if not downright false) degree of common experiences and interests. Obviously, not all women or members of ethnic minorities share similar experiences or hold similar values. Margaret Thatcher may have been Britain's first woman prime minister, but she was quite unsympathetic to what feminists defined as women's interests. Colin Powell was the most senior black person in the United States armed services in the early 1990s, but he served under Ronald Reagan, the most conservative president of the 20th century, and rarely associated himself with racial minority causes. One response of the partisan intellectual is to expel such people from the honoured group: Thatcher was not really a woman and Powell was an 'Uncle Tom'. The other response is to replace the diverse opinions of real people with what the analysts suppose they would have thought had their thinking not been distorted by ideology.

A further problem with partisanship is that the partisans often assume that all sociologists do (or should) share the same values. When he was president of the American Sociological Association, Michael Burawoy argued passionately for 'public sociology': sociology should stop pretending to be objective social science and should take sides. It should advocate on behalf of civil society and against authoritarian governments and neoliberal economies; it should, for example, support 'new social movements'. He does not specify exactly which new social movements should provide our guiding ideology. We can guess that he wants us to align with minority rights activists and environmentalists rather than with ethno-nationalists of the sort who became popular across the West in the first two decades of the 21st century, but nothing within the discipline justifies such narrow partisanship or justifies confining it to what suits the preferences of Californian academics.

Sociology is naturally and reasonably radical in the sense that its detached and detailed studies of social realities will often puncture the pretensions of those who punt idealized versions of what they are doing and why. But to be openly partisan means doing this only to individuals, classes, groups, institutions, and movements the partisans do not like, and such selectivity is a betrayal of the sociological calling.

Of course nothing should stop professional sociologists, as private citizens, using the results of their research as justification for political postures or as material for political persuasion. Nor should anything stop sociologists claiming that their opinions on matters on which they are genuinely expert should be taken more seriously than the opinions of others; that is, after all, what we mean by expertise. My assertion is the narrow one that partisanship in the conduct of sociological research and thought is to be resisted rather than encouraged or celebrated. The world has quite enough 'engaged voices' (sadly most of them without equally engaged brains) without those people who are in the fortunate position of being relatively free of external constraints abandoning any attempt at objectivity.

At this point I would like to defend the goal of objectivity. The partisans argue that value-neutral social science is impossible because sociologists cannot transcend their own ideologically constrained worldviews. If this point is not a statement of faith, it must be treated as a testable proposition. With only a little flippancy, I would note first that the partisans themselves refute their case: apparently ideology blinds others, but they manage to see through the mists. Unless the partisans can provide a plausible and testable explanation of their immunity, their intellectual good health offers good reason to doubt the prevalence and severity of the ailment from which the rest of us are supposed to suffer.

A second response is to note that, even if the non-sociological interests of researchers may distort some research findings, it may not distort all of them. To continue with the sickness metaphor, the illness might not impair all functions equally. To take my own work on Northern Ireland, the fact that I am Scottish rather than Irish might well have made me less sympathetic to Republican than to Loyalist terrorists, but it might have had no effect on my explanation of how terrorists attained leadership positions. The argument against objectivity supposes that contaminating bias distorts all one's work. My experience suggests that many interesting and important questions in sociology simply do not carry the moral, ethical, or political charge that would cause differences in observation and explanation to vary systematically with the social interests of those studying such questions.

Yet, even in cases where we might expect researchers to be biased, we still find sociologists taking positions that conflict with their personal preferences. I offer an example from the sociology of religion. Some sociologists believe that religion has declined markedly in the modern world; others believe that behind the apparent decline is an enduring and fairly constant religiosity that simply changes its mode of expression. Many sociologists of religion are themselves religious people and have been drawn to the discipline in order better to understand their own faith. So we might expect that the personal values of these commentators would influence how they see the evidence. But the protagonists do not line up as expected.

Among those persuaded by the evidence of secularization, we find two liberal atheists, a Lutheran, a former Methodist who became an ordained Anglican, a politically conservative atheist who mourned the passing of moral orthodoxy, an official of a major US denomination, and a professor in a conservative Baptist college. Those who believe that modern societies are almost every bit as religious as pre-industrial ones show a similarly broad range of religious positions. Especially when I observe that some of these scholars changed sides in the sociological battle without changing their religious beliefs, I conclude that this field at least shows that interests can be transcended or set aside. A similar case could be made from political sociology. Again we have scholars studying aspects of the social world in which they are personally involved and again we find no easy match between competing explanations of voting behaviour, for example, and political preferences.

A further response to the partisans is to observe that the quality of a body of scholarship does not depend solely on the personal virtues of scholars. As I noted for natural science, the social organization of the enterprise offers some protection against corruption from interests. Sociologists work in a competitive environment that allows the ready exchange of ideas and information. However blinkered I may be, there are others who are keen to prove me wrong. Objectivity does not depend on each of us being severally devoid of extra-disciplinary values; competition and collaboration neutralize the distorting effects of any one scholar's biases.

Finally, I would like to note that it is perfectly sensible to recognize that it is difficult to transcend one's own beliefs and values and still strive to overcome obstacles to objectivity. As the American economist Robert Solow nicely put it, we know that it is almost impossible to create an entirely germ-free environment, but most of us would rather have a heart operation in a modern operating theatre than in a sewer.

## Relativists

If one response to the problem of ideological contamination is frank partisanship, another is relativism, which brings me back to the subject of postmodernism. If reality is unknowable, if no objective and accurate account of the social world is possible, then we can do no more than endlessly manufacture partial descriptions of what the world looks like from this or that standpoint.

And none of those descriptions is superior to any other. Again what we see here is a complex interaction between aspects of the world as described by sociologists and the way in which some sociologists see their work. Relativism has become particularly popular among disciplines such as media studies and cultural studies that lie on the fringe of sociology, but, like cancer, it has fed secondaries throughout the body of the discipline and, like cancer, it needs to be eradicated if the discipline is to survive.

We can readily understand why relativism is popular in cultural studies. Although there are technical skills that can be evaluated and compared, whether Jane Austen is a better writer than Agatha Christie and John Constable a better painter than Jack Vettriano is largely a matter of taste. In most societies, the social hierarchy produces a hierarchy of tastes; one particular class decides what is good and bad art. In the Britain of the 1950s the expression 'I don't know much about art but I know what I like' was often attributed to some archetypically ill-educated lower-class person as a joke, a way of insulting a lack of sophistication. By the 1990s it had become an expression of high democratic principle. Attempts to preserve a 'canon' of good culture were seen as elitist folly. To suggest that Austen was a better writer than Christie came to be seen as snobbery.

In many Western democracies (the United States, in particular) attacks on cultural hierarchies took on a particularly bitter tone as they were attacked, not just for class, but also for gender and racial bias. High culture was dismissed as the work of 'dead white males'. While we might have some sympathy with such criticisms in art and literature, they raise the awkward question of just where one draws the line between what is legitimately a matter of personal preference and what is a matter of fact. Those who believe in rational thought and the possibility of social science should accord everyone the right to believe what they wish and yet reserve the right to argue that some beliefs are wrong: you have the right to believe that the world is run by giant green lizards and that the governments of the West are in regular contact with aliens, but I insist that such beliefs are not well founded.

What the relativist does is expand the realm of personal preference and hence of legitimate disagreement. The democracy of civil rights becomes a democracy of knowledge and that takes the form of supposing, not that everyone has an equal right of access to knowledge, but that what everyone believes is equally likely to be true. René Descartes's 'I think, therefore I am' becomes 'I believe, therefore I am right'.

Part of the appeal of relativism lies in its starkness: it is dramatic and clear, whereas the critical responses to it often seem mundane and unfocused. Fortunately, that does not stop them being good responses. They will not satisfy those who want simple and arresting formulas, but together they do form a comprehensive refutation of relativism.

A good place to begin is to distinguish between creation and discovery. It is true that explanations and theories (like all cultural products) are social constructions, but that does not mean that they invent the things they claim to discover. Newton discovered 'gravity', but prior to his intellectual activity people did not have trouble sticking to the earth's surface. He discovered it; he did not create it.

Another riposte is to note that contrary to the relativist's assertion that social explanations are mere narratives (and none better than any other), sociologists do often agree on evidence. Consensus is not itself proof; the alchemists shared common assumptions and methods, but their enterprise was still hokum. But where large numbers of scholars from disparate backgrounds come to similar conclusions, it becomes less easy to see their findings as collective delusion and easier to suppose that they are connecting with some external realities. That scholars from diverse backgrounds can agree suggests that there is a real world out there, independent of our beliefs about it, and hence that we can at least aspire to explore that world in a manner that is more than just an expression of personal preferences.

The point about understanding across cultural and social boundaries is important. If postmodernists are right that no reading, no account, has greater validity than any other, then communication beyond a small magic circle would be impossible. The whole notion of translation supposes that we can (at least in theory) distinguish between more and less correct translations. It may not be easy but the fact (and it is a 'fact') that nation-states negotiate treaties, that missionaries translate sacred scriptures into foreign languages, and that, every day, millions of us successfully communicate across class, gender, racial, ethnic, generational, and linguistic borders, should be enough to persuade us that the relativist's pessimism is misplaced.

Translation is possible because, for all the anthropological variation, there is much that is common in human experience. The perceptual and reasoning processes studied by psychologists are genuinely universal. No peoples anywhere in the globe have trouble counting their children or knowing when they are more, or less, hungry. One culture may have a strong preference for male offspring while another may treat baby boys and girls alike, but the joys and trials of parenthood are similar the world over. Cultures may differ in the way they like their beef. Westerners used to value fat cattle, now we prefer lean meat. But it is precisely because cattle rearers the world over share common understandings that they can compare the relative merits of lean over fat. For centuries the Masai of East Africa have raised cattle in the most hostile environments and one might suppose that they had little in common with the cattle breeders of the rich grasslands of the north-east of Scotland, but the first pedigree herd of Simmental cattle in Africa was founded in 1990 as a result of a collaboration between the Masai and a farmer from the Aberdeenshire village of Methlick. They were literally worlds apart, but they had a common love for cattle and could negotiate a common language for common action.

The difficulty with this sort of rejoinder to relativism is that relativists can refuse to be impressed because they reject the rules of engagement. Like the partisan who dismisses every criticism as mere ideology, the relativist can assert that the very idea of subjecting the claims of relativism to empirical test is based on an approach to knowledge that relativism shows to be mistaken.

The best answer to such blanket refusal to come to terms is to ask if relativists act consistently on their avowed philosophical position. Clearly they do not. Postmodernists write books and lecture; they try to communicate their claims to others. They do so because they believe that they are right and others are wrong. If they took a full-strength dose of their own medicine, they would shut up shop. If no reading is superior to any other, why destroy trees to announce that (especially for the umpteenth time) to the world? If it is not possible to distinguish truth from error, why do postmodernists argue with those who do not share their views?

## Statophobes

This may seem a strange topic to intrude at this stage, but there is a tendency in sociology which somewhat threatens the enterprise and it is partly driven by postmodern critiques of the scientific pretensions of social science. Sociology in the USA and in Germany seems less infected by this than British and French sociology (where anthropology and sociology have traditionally been institutionally close), but there is often an unstated linkage between arguing that the subject matter of sociology prevents it being scientific and arguing that to present social description in numbers, and to analyse it statistically, does damage to the essential nature of that subject matter.

There is no justification for avoiding numbers. All observation involves at least implicit counting: the anthropologist who describes one society as matrilineal and another as patrilineal has mentally counted up instances of actions and statements that show the relative importance of mothers and fathers, weighed the two piles, and chosen the appropriate label on the basis of the relative weights. Anyone who uses terms such as 'more' and 'less' is implicitly using numbers. Just as dividing musical tones (which are merely arbitrary points on a continuous scale of sound frequency) into distinct notes (as when we compare a G note with the A note one tone higher) involves some loss of information, so compressing complex observations into scales does mean that we lose something. But then so does the use of words, and unless we use an awful lot of words our descriptions will be nowhere near as accurate as those in numbers. Of course, the accuracy of numbers can sometimes be misleading and only a fool would make anything of small percentage differences, but any such drawback is more than compensated for by the utility of numbers and scales: they permit us to analyse far more data than do words.

Let us go back to the link between health and social class mentioned in Chapter 4. Assume that we have measures of health. How do we measure social class? We typically divide all occupations into five or seven grades and we may further simplify them into just two: white collar and blue collar or non-manual and manual work. We could add level of education. Experiences of education obviously vary enormously, but we typically bifurcate it by duration: school level and post-school level. We could describe wealth in very many ways, but usually we take stated income and divide it into two or three bands.

With every one of those operations we simplify, but the great benefit is that we can then compare the links between health and social class for thousands and even millions of people: numbers of cases that allow us to be confident that oddities and idiosyncrasies cancel out and so do not pervert the outcome. For most of our work, large datasets are necessary to identify the patterns which we wish to explain. Once we have established patterns we might wish to interview a small sample of people at great length to try to work out just how poverty, unemployment, or lack of education might explain ill health. We might start our research with some detailed ethnographies to point us in the right direction. But without the statistical analysis of large numbers of observations, expressed in numbers on scales, we cannot identify the patterns that social science hopes to explain.

## Zeitgeist philosophers

The penultimate threat to sociology I would like to identify comes, somewhat paradoxically, from social theory. Obviously, social science has to be interested in explanation and packages of interrelated explanations are often described as 'theory'. My problem is that much of the work that is discussed in books of social theory and social theory courses is not sociology. Many theorists are literary critics (Edward Said or Judith Butler, for example) or philosophers (for example, Michel Foucault), and what they offer is not proportionate generalization from well-evidenced research but sweeping generalization: in these cases, respectively, orientalism, performativity, or governmentality are presented as the master theme of modern life. Even those social theorists who are by training sociologists tend to be best known for snappy metaphors which aim to capture the essence of an epoch in a memorable word or phrase: Ulrich Beck on 'risk society', Zygmunt Baumann on 'liquid modernity', and Manuel Castells on 'network society', offer examples.

There is nothing wrong with big ideas. Historians who spent many years studying short time periods in small places may be offended by Durkheim's contrast of societies based on mechanical versus organic types of solidarity or by Ferdinand Tönnies's contrast of community versus voluntary association, but sociology properly differs from history in its ambition to generalize.

The problem with many of the currently popular zeitgeist metaphors is that they are too sweeping and have only the most shallow evidential roots. They are popular because they seem widely applicable but their apparently broad reach disguises a lack of specific application: with a bit of imagination, almost anything can be explained by liquid modernity. Glitzy metaphors will not help us understand our world. The best sociological theory is to be found a lot closer to empirical social research.

## Adjective sociologists

Finally, I return to a theme mentioned in the Preface: the unhelpfulness of sects within the discipline. It is common to find the noun 'sociology' preceded by an adjective; feminist sociology, political sociology, economic sociology, critical sociology, and the like. This could signify one of two things: one good and one bad. The adjective may simply describe a realm of social life or research agenda. It may be just a truncation of a longer phrase: the sociology of the polity becomes political sociology, a sociology which takes seriously gender differences becomes feminist sociology, the sociology of the economy becomes economic sociology. But it may instead mean that its proponents think that their kind of sociology requires different principles, different research techniques, and even different ethics.

We can see the point if we compare the sociology of religion (which is just sociology looking at religious institutions and behaviour) and religious sociology (which was popular with Catholics in the 1950s and 1960s and meant a sociology informed by Catholic Christian principles and harnessed in the service of promoting and improving Christianity). If feminist sociology simply means studying topics or asking questions which had been neglected until feminists eloquently argued their importance, it is a legitimate part of sociology's repertoire. If, as is sometimes argued, it means avoiding surveys and statistics because they are patriarchal, knowing one's conclusions before the research is started, and putting political change before accurate description and explanation, then it is no more legitimate than Christian sociology or Muslim sociology. If critical sociology means studying topics that governments would rather we ignored or asking unpopular questions about power, it is a legitimate part of our enterprise. If it means espousing Marxist politics, it is no more legitimate than fascist or totalitarian sociology.

## The nature of sociology

In this short book it would have been impossible to describe sociology by comprehensively listing the impressive contributions to our understanding of the world that have been produced by the discipline's practitioners. I have tried to make some reference to the major figures and their most significant contributions: Marx and Weber on class; Weber on rationality; Durkheim on anomie; Gehlen on instincts; Merton on the structural causes of crime; Mead and Cooley on socialization; Michels on oligarchy; Parsons on the family; Becker on labelling; and Goffman on roles and total institutions. I have also tried to mention sufficient empirical sociological studies to give some idea of what sociologists do. However, the text has been designed to present a sense, not a summary, of sociology.

If sociology is to be anything more than speculation, it has to be *empirical*. That is, its explanations (and their packaging in theories) must be based on sound observations of the real world. Hence my selection of scholars has leant towards those who have combined theory with detailed studies. If it is to be empirical, then sociology must model itself on the natural sciences.

However, in asserting that sociology must be a social science, we must also bear in mind the peculiar disadvantages and advantages that come from the discipline's odd subject matter: we study ourselves. The capacities of reasoning and interpreting that allow us to do more than act out drives provided by our instincts and respond to our physical environment are also what allow us to study anything. In turn this means that we cannot hope to treat social action as the symptoms of underlying regularities akin to the laws of the physical world. We have to recognize the socially constructed nature of reality and study those social constructions (of which sociology is itself a particular systematized and refined example). For the partisan and the relativist this is a conundrum to which we can respond only by abandoning social science and taking sides on ideological grounds (the partisan view) or taking all sides or none (the relativist position).

As I have argued, both of these forms of surrender are an unnecessarily pessimistic reaction to the discipline's unusual subject matter. It is certainly not easy to understand the causes of crime or the decline of religion in the West, nor to explain political preferences and educational attainment. But so long as, in our everyday lives, we continue to believe we can work out which buses go to the town centre, which churches offer to hear confessions, which political parties come closest to our preferences, and when our children are lying to us, I see no reason why we should believe that the systematic examination of such questions on a larger scale is impossible.

At various places in the text I have drawn attention to the ways in which sociological explanations differ from common sense: sociology recognizes the socially constructed nature of reality; it identifies the hidden causes of action; it describes the unanticipated consequences of action. But I would also assert that common sense itself provides the best warrant for the possibility of social science. Some of us are better at it than others and we all make mistakes, but every day, in hundreds of small ways, we observe, describe, understand, and explain our actions and the actions of others. If we can do it as amateurs, I see no reason why, with greater effort, we cannot do it professionally.

# References

## Chapter 2: Social constructions

Durkheim quote: Émile Durkheim, *Suicide: A Study in Sociology*. Trans. J. A. Spaulding and G. Simpson (London: Routledge & Kegan Paul, 1970), 246.
Ibid., 248.
Sartre quote is from Erving Goffman, *The Presentation of Self in Everyday Life* (New York: Overlook Press, 1973), 75.

## Chapter 4: The modern world

Marshall quote: Gordon Marshall, *In Praise of Sociology* (London: Routledge, 1992), 29.

# Further reading

There are very many comprehensive introductory textbooks. My current UK favourite is James Fulcher and John Scott, *Sociology* (Oxford: Oxford University Press, 2016).

The theoretical issues explored in Chapter 2 are ably treated in Peter L. Berger and Thomas Luckmann, *The Social Construction of Reality* (Harmondsworth: Penguin, 1976). It is in parts a difficult read, but the main ideas appear in briefer and more accessible form in Peter L. Berger, *Invitation to Sociology* (Harmondsworth: Penguin, 1990). The relationship between the individual and society also forms the main theme of Laurie Taylor and Stan Cohen, *Escape Attempts: The Theory and Practice of Resistance to Everyday Life* (London: Routledge, 1992).

The description of modern societies summarized in Chapter 4 owes a great deal to Ernest Gellner, *Plough, Sword and Book: The Structure of Human History* (London: Paladin, 1986), which, in under 300 pages and in admirably clear prose, explains the shifts from hunter-gatherer to agrarian to industrial societies.

The classics are regularly reprinted, and, while Marx is both difficult and passé, Weber and Durkheim are still eminently readable. So I would recommend H. H. Gerth and C. Wright Mills (eds), *From Max Weber: Essays in Sociology* (London: Routledge, 1991), and Émile Durkheim, *Suicide: A Study in Sociology* (London: Routledge, 1970).

There are so many modern works that deserve to be classics that it is invidious to select just a few, but the following from the 1950s and 1960s combine acute observation and sociological reasoning to exemplify the best traditions of the discipline:

Becker, Howard, *Outsiders* (London: Free Press, 1963).

Dalton, Melville, *Men Who Manage: Fusions of Feeling and Theory in Administration* (London: John Wiley & Sons, 1959).

Goffman, Erving, *The Presentation of Self in Everyday Life* (Harmondsworth: Penguin, 1969).

Gouldner, Alvin, *Wildcat Strike* (London: Routledge & Kegan Paul, 1957).

Lockwood, David, *The Blackcoated Worker* (London: Allen & Unwin, 1958).

Young, Michael, and Willmott, Peter, *Family and Kinship in East London* (Harmondsworth: Penguin, 1961).

Since the 1960s the higher-education sector of all industrial societies has expanded massively, and with it the number of sociologists. The growth and increased specialization of the discipline have made it increasingly difficult for any studies to become known outside their particular field, but the following are fine examples of very different styles of empirical work:

Bourdieu, Pierre, *Distinction: A Social Critique of the Judgement of Taste* (London: Routledge, 2010).

Hochschild, Arlie Russell, *The Second Shift: Working Parents and the Revolution at Home* (Harmondsworth: Penguin, 2012).

Wilkinson, Richard and Pickett, Kate, *The Spirit Level: Why Equality is Better for Everyone* (Harmondsworth: Penguin, 2010).

# Publisher's acknowledgements

We are grateful for permission to include the following copyright material in this book.

Extracts from Émile Durkheim, *Suicide: A Study in Sociology*. Trans. J. A. Spaulding and G. Simpson (London: Routledge & Kegan Paul, 1970), 246, 248.

Approximately one hundred and twenty-one (121) words from THE PRESENTATION OF SELF IN EVERYDAY LIFE by Erving Goffman (Anchor Books 1959, Penguin Press 1969, Pelican Books 1971, Penguin Books 1990). Copyright (c) Erving Goffman 1959.

The publisher and author have made every effort to trace and contact all copyright holders before publication. If notified, the publisher will be pleased to rectify any errors or omissions at the earliest opportunity.

# Index

# SOCIAL MEDIA
# Very Short Introduction

# Join our community
www.oup.com/vsi

- Join us online at the official Very Short Introductions **Facebook** page.
- Access the thoughts and musings of our authors with our online **blog**.
- Sign up for our monthly **e-newsletter** to receive information on all new titles publishing that month.
- Browse the full range of Very Short Introductions online.
- Read **extracts** from the Introductions for free.
- If you are a teacher or lecturer you can order inspection copies quickly and simply via our website.

# ADVERTISING
## A Very Short Introduction
Winston Fletcher

The book contains a short history of advertising and an
explanation of how the industry works, and how each of the
parties (the advertisers , the media and the agencies) are
involved. It considers the extensive spectrum of advertisers
and their individual needs. It also looks at the financial side of
advertising and asks how advertisers know if they have been
successful, or whether the money they have spent has in fact
been wasted. Fletcher concludes with a discussion about the
controversial and unacceptable areas of advertising such as
advertising products to children and advertising products such
as cigarettes and alcohol. He also discusses the benefits of
advertising and what the future may hold for the industry.

# INFORMATION
## A Very Short Introduction
Luciano Floridi

Luciano Floridi, a philosopher of information, cuts across many subjects, from a brief look at the mathematical roots of information - its definition and measurement in 'bits'- to its role in genetics (we are information), and its social meaning and value. He ends by considering the ethics of information, including issues of ownership, privacy, and accessibility; copyright and open source. For those unfamiliar with its precise meaning and wide applicability as a philosophical concept, 'information' may seem a bland or mundane topic. Those who have studied some science or philosophy or sociology will already be aware of its centrality and richness. But for all readers, whether from the humanities or sciences, Floridi gives a fascinating and inspirational introduction to this most fundamental of ideas.

'Splendidly pellucid.'

Steven Poole, The Guardian

www.oup.com/vsi

# ONLINE CATALOGUE
## A Very Short Introduction

Our online catalogue is designed to make it easy to find your ideal Very Short Introduction. View the entire collection by subject area, watch author videos, read sample chapters, and download reading guides.